AF477160

TEEN STUDY BIBLE FOR BOYS

52-week Teen Bible Guide for Boys

By

Anders Bennett

ADISAN Publishing AB

© 2021 by ADISAN Publishing AB, Sweden

No part of this publication may be reproduced, stored in a retrieval system, or transmitted in any form or by any means, electronic, mechanical, photocopying, recording, scanning, or otherwise, as permitted under sections 107 and 108 of the 1976 United States Copyright Act, without the prior permission of the Publisher.

All scripture quotations, unless otherwise indicated, are taken from the HOLY BIBLE, NEW INTERNATIONAL VERSION®, NIV®. Copyright © 1973, 1978, 1984, 2011 by Biblica, Inc. ™ used by permission. All rights reserved
World Wide.

Limit of Liability/ Disclaimer of Warranty: The publisher and the author make no representations or warranties concerning the accuracy or completeness of this work's content and expression. Neither the Publisher nor the author shall be liable for damages arising herewith.

TABLE OF CONTENTS

Introduction 1

How to Read This Study Bible 2

Week 1: Who Am I? 4

Week 2: Christ Alone, Cornerstone 7

Week 3: The Greatest Commandment 10

Week 4: The Great Commission 13

Week 5: Being a Good Sport 16

Week 6: Body Image 19

Week 7: Stress and Anxiety 22

Week 8: Getting in Spiritual Shape 25

Week 9: Servant Leadership 28

Week 10: Don't Complain 31

Week 11: Honoring your Parents 34

Week 12: Being a Godly Brother 37

Week 13: Consider Your Source 40

Week 14: The Holy Spirit 43

Week 15: Your Will Be Done 46

Week 16: Actions Speak Louder than Words 49

Week 17: The Company We Keep 52

Week 18: Bullies 55

Week 19: Forgiving Others 58

Week 20: Life Without Filters 61

Week 21: Listen! 64

Week 22: Worship 67

Week 23: Worshipping God through School 70

Week 24: Integrity 73

Week 25: Doubt Is Okay 76

Week 26: The Gift of Singleness 79

Week 27: Date Intentionally 82

Week 28: How to be a Good Boyfriend 85

Week 29: Why Wait? 88

Week 30: How to be a Witness... 91

Week 31: Friendship 94

Week 32: You're Better Than That... 97

Week 33: God is Sovereign.. 100

Week 34: Grief is Okay 103

Week 35: Evangelism.. 106

Week 36: What Goes in Must Come Out 109

Week 37: Breakups 112

Week 38: Who's Your Master?.. 115

Week 39: Wise Guys... 118

Week 40: Positive Peer Pressure.. 121

Week 41: How to Love the Jerks.. 124

Week 42: Standing Firm for God... 127

Week 43: The Blessing of Your Words 130

Week 44: No Offense 133

Week 45: Dealing with Conflict... 136

Week 46: The Least of These.. 139

Week 47: God is Always with Us... 142

Week 48: Life on Hard Mode... 145

Week 49: Enjoying Salvation Today 148

Week 50: Giving to God... 151

Week 51: A failure is Sometimes an Option 154

Week 52: Our Home in Heaven.. 157

Conclusion.. 160

INTRODUCTION

"The thief comes only to steal and kill and destroy; I have come that they may have life, and have it to the full."

John 10:10

"Life" is one of God's greatest gifts to us, his beloved creations. Every day there is so much life to enjoy and blessings from God to experience. Sure, there is plenty in this world that is harsh, tough, and not at all fun, to say the least. Despite the sin that may be around us, as John 10:10 states, Jesus came so that we can experience *Life to the fullest*.

Being a teenager can be one of the most difficult experiences in the world. You are growing and changing physically, emotionally, and spiritually every day. As you are growing, you are met with new experiences, some of which are exciting, and others can be terrifying. You are at the age where you are beginning to ask really important questions.

Who am I? What should I be doing with my life? Who are my people? Where is God?

And the list goes on. It's easy to become stressed by all the questions that come our way, which can distract us from enjoying the full life that Jesus wants us to experience, but I have wonderful news for you!

You don't have to live life alone! God is with you every day and wants to have a deep and meaningful relationship with YOU! Living life with God and finding strength and power in His Word, the Bible is one of the most important ways to experience this full and wonderful life that Jesus wants us to have.

This book is meant to help be a connection between YOU and GOD. I pray that the Holy Spirit moves through these devotionals, the scripture you read each day, the prayers, and reflection questions to help deepen your relationship with God.

Connecting with God is the key to being able to experience your best life possible. We hope you use these devotions to come to God with all your joys, concerns, prayers, and questions. There is nothing better than spending time with God, and we are excited to be able to help you experience that blessing.

HOW TO READ THIS STUDY BIBLE

This Devotional is broken up into four sections. Each is uniquely designed to help you experience God in a different method. In this devotional, you will be experiencing God through the Bible, through prayer, through the thoughts of others, and even by reflecting on your own life.

As you read this devotional, we suggest that you find a quiet place where you can peacefully and easily feel comfortable spending time with God. Maybe it's your room or a back porch. Maybe it's your favorite couch in your living room, or it's in your car before you go to school every day. Wherever it is, we suggest you find a great time and place to be able to spend time with God every day.

Here is how each devotional is broken down each week:

Weekly Devotional: Each week, the devotional will have a theme, or a thought, to help guide you in your time with God. The devotional will be a short reading intended to get you thinking about the topic of the week and how it applies to your life. It is our prayer that the Holy Spirit moves through the words and connects with the parts of your life that God wants to move through.

Reflection Question: After you read the devotion, you will be asked two deep questions to help connect the topic you read about to your daily life. These are questions about YOUR life, so there is no real wrong answer. That being said, they will challenge you to think deeply and critically about your life, how you act, and what you think about certain topics. Don't worry; nobody has ever died from thinking too deeply!

Prayer: At the end of each devotional, there will be a prayer that we have prayed for you and that we ask that you pray for yourself. You can pray it out loud or in your head. You can choose to pray it every day of the week or just after you read the devotion. This is your time to communicate with God personally, so feel free to add to the prayer with your own words if you'd like!

Daily Scripture: Lastly, perhaps most importantly, each day of the week, we have asked you to read a section of scripture that connects with the weekly topic. Each scripture has been picked because it is relative to the theme. Studying God's word is the best way to grow in your faith and knowledge of who God made you to be. We encourage you to make a point to read each daily scripture and allow the Holy Spirit to use these powerful words to shape who you are.

As you look through the devotions, you may realize that these readings won't take you very long each day. That's okay! We are confident that even if you spend just a little time in the Bible and conversing with God daily, you will be opening the doors to allow the Holy Spirit to transform your heart in big ways.

Whether you're a teenager reading this book or the adults who wrote it, there is nothing more important in life than having a relationship with God. This book serves as a tool to help you grow in your relationship with your Heavenly Father. We hope it helps and pray that the Holy Spirit moves through this little book in BIG ways!

WEEK 1: WHO AM I?

Reading Plan for NIV Scriptures:

DAY 1: ROMANS 8:14-16 *(You are a child of God)*

DAY 2: EPHESIANS 5:1-7 *(You are a child of Light)*

DAY 3: JOHN 1:9-13 *(We are God's children because of Jesus)*

DAY 4: GENESIS 1:26-27 *(We are made in God's image)*

DAY 5: GALATIANS 3:26-29 *(We are Heirs according to God's promise)*

DAY 6: 1 JOHN 3:1-10 *(Children of God live pure lives)*

DAY 7: 1 PETER 2:4-10 *(You are part of a chosen people, a royal priesthood)*

WEEKLY COMMENTARY:

Who are you?

As a teenager, you are at the age where you are just now beginning to answer this question for yourself, and it's okay if you don't have the complete answer figured out yet.

When you answer the question, *"Who am I?"* How do you respond? Perhaps you list your name, age, and what school you attend. Maybe you mention what sports you play or what activities you are part of. Maybe you reference your family or circle of friends as a defining point of *who you are*.

These are all important factors in your life, but make no mistake, they do not define *who you are*.

Your identity is NOT found in what you do, who you are related to, or even your successes and failures. The answer to the three-word question, "Who am I" is found in three other words. You are a Child of God.

Take a moment and let those words soak in. Say it to yourself. Read this sentence out loud.

"I am a Child of God."

The Bible says that we are made in God's image. That means when you look in the mirror and see yourself; you are looking at a reflection of who God is. The Bible calls us heirs and a royal priesthood. You read that correctly...in the eyes of God, we are considered *royalty*!

God, the most powerful, perfect, and almighty being that exists, has ever existed, or ever will exist, look at YOU and calls you "My child." Knowing this should influence everything about how you see yourself and live your life.

Being a child of God means you are free to live a holy life that honors God. Being part of God's family means that Jesus has died for your sins, and evil has no more power in your life. You are not defined by temporary things like what activity you do, what grades you get, or what mistakes you have made. You are defined by the fact that you are loved by your Heavenly Father and Creator.

REFLECTION QUESTIONS:

Who do you, or people you know, say that you are?

____
____
____
____
____
____
____

How does being loved, accepted, and chosen by God shape your identity and daily decisions?

____
____
____
____
____
____
____
____

PRAYER

Dear Jesus, thank you so much for accepting me and calling me out of darkness and into your marvelous light. God, help me find strength in my identity as your chosen and loved child, and please guide me with your Holy Spirit to live my life in a way that honors this amazing blessing. Thank you for loving me and making me in Your image. Amen.

WEEK 2: CHRIST ALONE, CORNERSTONE

Reading Plan for NIV Scriptures:

DAY 1: 📖 1 PETER 2:4-5 *(We are holy because of Jesus)*

DAY 2: 📖 LUKE 6:46-49 *(Jesus's teaching are our solid foundation)*

DAY 3: 📖 PHILIPPIANS 4:13 *(We can do all things because of Christ)*

DAY 4: 📖 JOHN 3:16-17 *(God saved the world through Jesus Christ)*

DAY 5: 📖 ROMANS 8:1-2 *(We are free because of Jesus)*

DAY 6: 📖 COLOSSIANS 2:9-14 *(Christ alone died for our sins)*

DAY 7: 📖 EPHESIANS 2:19-22 *(Christ is our Cornerstone)*

WEEKLY COMMENTARY:

The *cornerstone* is the first stone used in constructing buildings back in Biblical times. It was the stone used to measure the rest of the architecture, and often if something happened to the cornerstone, the entire building was in jeopardy. That was never a serious worry for builders, though, because they had faith in the strength and security of the cornerstone.

When we say that Jesus is our cornerstone, the same truths apply. As Christians, Jesus is the center of everything that our faith and religion are built on. Take a moment and think about how *foundational* Jesus is to our faith.

Jesus died on the cross for your sins; without Jesus, you would still have a sin-shaped wedge between you and God. The Bible tells us that only Jesus could take on the burden of our sins, and there isn't a single person on earth that could bear that weight on their own.

Jesus also provides us with the perfect role model of how to live a Christian life. God sent his Son to live a holy and perfect life here on Earth so that we would have an example of how to be the best versions of ourselves. Jesus's teaching is essential to our development.

Jesus offers you the freedom that only He can offer. Not only did he die for your sins so you don't have to spend eternity in Hell, but Jesus also died for your sins so that they don't have to weigh you down today. Any sin that you're dealing with today know that Jesus already died for it. You're essentially holding on to deadweight and something that has no real power over you, thanks to Jesus.

Even though it may feel like sin has power over you, thanks to the blood of Jesus Christ, it does not.

This week I hope you find strength in the fact that Christ is your cornerstone. You can do all things through Him who gives you strength, and you can overcome all things as well. Take time this week, and thank Jesus for being your firm foundation.

REFLECTION QUESTIONS:

What is a sin that you are struggling with that you want to give to Jesus this week? Is there anything holding you back from doing so? If yes, what is it?

____
____
____
____
____
____
____
____

How is your life better because of Jesus Christ? Take time this week to take account of all the blessings you have because of everything that Jesus has done for you.

____
____
____
____
____
____
____
____

PRAYER:

Thank you, Jesus, my rock. Thank you for dying on the cross for me and taking my sins upon yourself. Thank you for living the perfect life and giving me an example that I can model my life after. Help me, Lord, to look to you for strength and support every day, no matter what my circumstances may be. Amen.

WEEK 3: THE GREATEST COMMANDMENT

Reading Plan for NIV Scriptures:

DAY 1: MATTHEW 22:33-40 *(Love God, love Others)*

DAY 2: 1 JOHN 4:7-12 *(God is love)*

DAY 3: DEUTERONOMY 6:5 *(Love the Lord with everything)*

DAY 4: 1 PETER 3:8-9 *(Don't repay evil with evil)*

DAY 5: JOHN 14:15 *(Love God by keeping His commands)*

DAY 6: LUKE 10:29-37 *(Love by taking care of others)*

DAY 7: HEBREWS 13:15-16 *(Loving others is worship to God)*

WEEKLY COMMENTARY:

I'm a relatively simple guy. I like things easy and to the point. If there is a way to do something that involves only one or two steps, I am here for it. In school, when the teacher used to say, "If you only remember one thing…remember this!" I took that as permission to only remember the one thing they were about to say and forget everything else.

The Bible has a lot of information in it, and all of it can benefit our lives. There's a lot. The history of the church, all kinds of rules and guidelines, suggestions, wisdom, poetry. It can often feel overwhelming. In Matthew 22, Jesus summed up everything in a two-part command.

> **37** *Jesus replied: "'Love the Lord your God with all your heart and with all your soul and with all your mind.'[c]* **38** *This is the first and greatest commandment.* **39** *And the second is like it: 'Love your neighbor as yourself.'[d]* **40** *All the Law and the Prophets hang on these two commandments."*

Matthew 22:37-40

Jesus tells us that if we only can remember to do but two things as Christians, it should be to love God and love others.

Loving God is the most important and best and most effective way to show your love to God, which is by loving His creation. So by loving other people, you're loving God!

As a teenager, you are beginning to ask yourself really hard questions. What are you going to do after high school? What are you going to do after school today? What do you want to do with your life? Who are you going to grow up to be? What is God's plan for you, and how does that answer all these questions?

The good news is that with God's help and in God's time, you'll be able to eventually answer all of those questions. Sometimes it takes a while, and you may not always be sure, but here's some more good news. Even if you don't know every step of your life plan, as long as you love God and love others, you are doing what God wants you to do.

REFLECTION QUESTIONS:

What are at least five ways that you can LOVE GOD this week?

____
____
____
____
____
____
____
____

What are five ways you can LOVE OTHER PEOPLE this week?

____
____
____
____
____
____
____
____

PRAYER:

God, thank you so much for loving me so much that you sent your Son to die on the cross for me, and you provide for me daily. Help me every day to grow in my own love for you, and help me find ways to show it. Also, please help me as I strive to love everyone in my life, especially the people that are hard to love. Help me this week to show love to someone who I feel doesn't deserve it. Amen!

WEEK 4: THE GREAT COMMISSION

Reading Plan for NIV Scriptures:

DAY 1: MATTHEW 28:18-20 *(Jesus commands us to go and make disciples)*

DAY 2: MATTHEW 5:13-16 *(We are salt and light in this world)*

DAY 3: GALATIANS 6:9-10 *(Do good to all people)*

DAY 4: ACTS 13:47 *(We are a light to those that don't know God)*

DAY 5: MARK 16:15 *(We are called to go and preach)*

DAY 6: ACTS 20:24 *(Nothing is more important than sharing Jesus)*

DAY 7: PSALM 105:1 *(Praise God by proclaiming his name)*

WEEKLY COMMENTARY:

If the President of the United States came to your house today with a specific task in mind, you would take it seriously, wouldn't you? You wouldn't just blow it off. A world leader paid YOU a visit with a job, so you'd probably be inclined to do it and do it well!

If the principal of your school called you in for a very important task and requested you specifically for the job, you probably wouldn't ditch that meeting, right? Hopefully, you would go learn what you need to do, and then you would complete your job to the best of your ability.

How much more important is Jesus as your leader than a principal and president?

In Matthew 28, Jesus gives us a command so important that we came up with a new word for it to set it apart. It's not Jesus's command; it's his Commission. You know this will be important because Jesus starts his Commission by saying, "All authority on heaven and earth has been given to me."

That's all the authority. Jesus states to us that he has all the authority, and then he gives us this commission, "Go and make disciples."

The Greek word used here for "Go" can also be translated as "As you are going." So read it again like this, "As you are going, make disciples."

We should try to make disciples of Jesus in everything we do. As you go to school, make disciples. As you are hanging with your friends, make disciples. As you're at church, make disciples. When you're home, make disciples. You get the picture. Wherever you are, look for opportunities to make disciples.

Look at your surroundings with fresh eyes this week, asking, "As I go, where can I make disciples?"

REFLECTION QUESTIONS:

What does it mean to you to "Make Disciples"? What are things you can do to make disciples? *(This is a great question to also ask a pastor, your parents, or any kind of Christian mentor you have)*

____

____

____

____

____

____

____

____

Where do you go? Where are the most common places you are at, and who are the people you could be sharing Jesus with?

____

____

____

____

____

____

____

____

PRAYER:

Thank you, God, for always being with me. Please help guide me in all the places I go to strive to make disciples in everything I do and every conversation I have. Direct my words into conversations about you, and then give me the right things to say. Help me live my life in a way that people see you and want to learn more about you. Amen.

WEEK 5: BEING A GOOD SPORT

Reading Plan for NIV Scriptures:

DAY 1: 📖 PROVERBS 24:17-18 *(Don't gloat)*

DAY 2: 📖 PHILIPPIANS 2:3-5 *(Do nothing out of selfish ambition)*

DAY 3: 📖 2 TIMOTHY 2:5 *(Follow the rules)*

DAY 4: 📖 PROVERBS 25:28 *(Exhibit Self Control)*

DAY 5: 📖 ROMANS 15:2 *(Build others up)*

DAY 6: 📖 GALATIANS 5:22-23 *(Fruit of the Spirit traits)*

DAY 7: 📖 PHILIPPIANS 3:14 *(Your true goal is Christ Jesus)*

WEEKLY COMMENTARY:

When I was younger, I hated when adults told me, "You're a good sport." Usually, this compliment followed a situation that I didn't want to have happened. We just lost a game, and someone told me I am a good sport. I was asked not to play so somebody (probably better) could, and when I agreed, they told me I was a good sport.

Looking back, I can honestly say in most things; I don't think there is much more important than "being a good sport." Your behavior and attitude before and after your win or loss are often more important than the game's outcome or performance. We have phases like "Nobody likes a sore loser." Perhaps you have had an exceptionally talented friend at a game or activity that you all stopped inviting to hang out with because they are the worst winners ever.

In Hollywood, there are plenty of fantastic actors that can't get work because directors refuse to work with them because of their attitude. It doesn't matter if it's a sport, in a musical, at work, or hanging out with your friends or family, being a good sport about all things can really help you earn favor among people, and it makes you more pleasant to be around.

Just so we're clear, here are some qualities of being a good sport. You are honest and don't lie to get ahead. You take losing well and respectfully, and you don't gloat or brag when you win. You are kind in all situations, whether things are going well or not. You don't get angry or hateful if you have an issue with others.

Did you notice that every quality I mentioned about good sportsmanship is also qualities of being a Christlike Christian? When we show good sportsmanship in everything we do, we are also showing Jesus in everything we do.

When you win, use it as an opportunity to share Jesus in how you act. If you lose, you still have an opportunity to win by sharing Jesus with how you accept the loss. Throughout the whole game, performance, shift at work, or overall experience, share God with others by how you treat them and how you are a joy to be around.

Being a good sport is actually a really good thing to be!

REFLECTION QUESTIONS:

What does Good Sportsmanship mean to you? What are the qualities of being a good sport?

____
____
____
____
____
____
____
____

Would you consider yourself a good sport? How well do you take your losses? How do you act when you win? Are there any areas in Good Sportsmanship that you could work on this week?

____
____
____
____
____
____
____
____

PRAYER:

God, please help me share with you how I live in all circumstances. When I win, please let me use that as an opportunity to point others to you. When I lose, please help me lose respectfully in a way that doesn't deter others from you. Help me always be respectful to my teammates and competition, and share love and grace with everyone I come into contact with.
Amen.

WEEK 6: BODY IMAGE

Reading Plan for NIV Scriptures:

DAY 1: 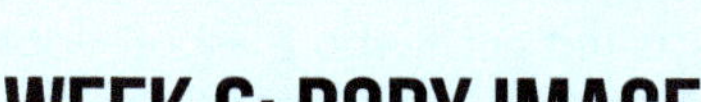 EPHESIANS 1:11 *(You are chosen)*

DAY 2: PHILIPPIANS 1:6 *(God does good work in you)*

DAY 3: 1 SAMUEL 16:7 *(God looks at the heart)*

DAY 4: 1 TIMOTHY 4:4 *(Everything God created is good)*

DAY 5: EPHESIANS 2:10 *(We are God's handiwork)*

DAY 6: 2 CORINTHIANS 5:17 *(You are a new creation in Christ)*

DAY 7: 1 CORINTHIANS 15:10 *(By the grace of God you are who you are)*

WEEKLY COMMENTARY:

What are your first thoughts when you look at yourself in the mirror? Do you like what you see? Or does your mind immediately remind you of all the changes you could make if you could? Statistically, most people your age struggle with body image and are unsatisfied with who they see looking back at them in the mirror.

This kind of thinking is not from God.

God made each and every one of us and didn't make a single mistake in Creation. A friend of mine phrases it, "God has never made a mistake, and that includes when He made you." The Bible calls us "chosen" and a "royal priesthood." We are considered "Good work" and "God's handiwork." What's more, whereas it's easy for us to judge ourselves and one another based on what we see on the outside, God finds value in what's on the inside.

There is so much more to you than what meets the eye. Your eyes often tell you that you're not good enough, but in the eyes of God, you are a masterpiece.

Too often, we go through our weeks comparing ourselves to the other people in our life. "I wish I was as muscular as him," or "I wish I was as thin as that guy." or "I am not nearly as good-looking as these other people I know." Don't think like that...you are a masterpiece that was intentionally made by God, the Author and Creator of Everything!

This week I challenge you to take pride in what you see in the mirror every morning. Instead of telling yourself, "Well, this is what we're working with today," try to remind yourself, "I am God's handiwork," or "I'm a masterpiece created by God."

Learn to love your body because God intentionally designed you and loves you so very much!

REFLECTION QUESTIONS:

What is your honest opinion about your body? What are your favorite parts? What would you change if you could?

____
____
____
____
____
____
____
____

How would you say that God views you? How can learning to love yourself like God loves you change how you view parts of yourself that are harder to love?

____
____
____
____
____
____
____
____

PRAYER:

God, thank you for creating me and loving me every single day. Please help me learn to view myself and others the way that you view your creations. Help me learn to love everything about my image and learn to not want to change anything about myself. Everything you do is on purpose, including how you created me. Thank you for creating me the way I am.
Amen.

WEEK 7: STRESS AND ANXIETY

Reading Plan for NIV Scriptures:

DAY 1: 📖 1 PETER 5:6-7 *(Cast your anxiety on God)*

DAY 2: 📖 PSALM 94:17-19 *(God brings you joy even when you're anxious)*

DAY 3: 📖 ROMANS 8:38-39 *(Nothing can separate us from God)*

DAY 4: 📖 MATTHEW 10:29-31 *(If God takes care of birds, He'll take care of you)*

DAY 5: 📖 HEBREWS 13:5-6 *(Don't be afraid, the Lord is your helper)*

DAY 6: 📖 PSALM 34:17 *(God will deliver you from your troubles)*

DAY 7: 📖 MATTHEW 6:25 *(Don't worry about your life)*

WEEKLY COMMENTARY:

As a teenager, you are experiencing so many new things at once. Your body is changing, you are in new environments, and you are constantly trying things that you have never done before. New activities, new teachers, new friends, new schools, there are so many new experiences. Some of them are wonderful, and some are the absolute worst. And we're all built differently, so what is true for your family or friends may or may not be true for you.

I remember, as a teenager, being stressed about my grades, if a particular girl liked me, what my friends and classmates thought of me, if I could be good enough at all my activities, and if I was making my parents proud. All that stress was exhausting, especially when you take into account the physical and biological growth that's happening with your body, which is also proven scientifically to be exhausting as well.

Believe me, when I tell you, life gets 100% better. If you are dealing with stress and anxiety now, please keep pushing through to the better times that will for sure be happening in your life! It's rare that you hear an adult say, "my teenage years were the best time of my life."

So what can you do in the intense stress and anxiety that your teenage years will bring you? The short answer, lean on God and lean on others.

Sometimes in our hardest times, it's easy to feel all alone, but please know that you are never alone. No matter how bad things may seem or how stressful life gets, God is more powerful than anything you deal with.

You'll still have to go through it, but you get to go with God.

It's also important to note that one of the ways that God helps us through the stress of life is by providing us with our family, friends, and sometimes even medical help. Don't feel bad if your anxiety ever gets to the point where you need professional help. God provided those doctors and medicine as an outlet to help us. Who are the people in your life that you can count on during stressful times? Who are your prayer partners or venting buddies? Talking about your stress may not fix the issues, but you'll feel better!

Life is stressful, but you don't have to deal with the stress alone. Dealing with your anxiety with God is much better than trying to get through it by yourself!

REFLECTION QUESTIONS:

What are the current stresses in your life that are making you the most anxious?

____
____
____
____
____
____
____
____

What are healthy ways to deal with your stress and anxiety? Who are the people that God has given you to help get you through stressful times? How is it easier to deal with your stress with God's help?

____
____
____
____
____
____
____
____

PRAYER:

Lord, I want to take this time to give you all my stressful situations and everything that is currently making me anxious. Whenever I feel like it's more then I can bear, I know that you are here with me and that you can bear all things. Since you can bear everything, and you are here with me, I know that because of you, I can bear all things too. I pray for strength, and I pray for peace. Amen!

WEEK 8: GETTING IN SPIRITUAL SHAPE

Reading Plan for NIV Scriptures:

DAY 1: 📖 MARK 1:35 *(Jesus set time apart in his day for prayer)*

DAY 2: 📖 EXODUS 20:8-11 *(Keep the Sabbath holy)*

DAY 3: 📖 1 CORINTHIANS 9:24-27 *(Spiritual fitness is greater than physical fitness)*

DAY 4: 📖 HEBREWS 5:11-14 *(Spiritual maturity is important)*

DAY 5: 📖 1 TIMOTHY 4:7-8 *(Train yourself to be godly)*

DAY 6: 📖 JOSHUA 1:8 *(Meditate on Scripture every day)*

DAY 7: 📖 1 THESSALONIANS 5:16-18 *(Rejoice, pray, and give thanks constantly)*

WEEKLY COMMENTARY:

Practice Makes Perfect

We try to live this slogan out in everything we do. If you take music lessons, you probably play your instrument every day, learning the pieces for next week's lesson. If you're on a sports team, you are working out every day and doing regular practices to learn new plays and ensure your body is in the best possible shape for your sport. It takes discipline to make ourselves good at anything and everything.

And your walk with God is no different.

There is no mystery or secret in how to grow in our faith and spiritual life. Regular prayer, scripture reading, attending church, reading devotionals like this, godly community, fasting, worship, and so much more. Remember the Sabbath and take time away from your crazy busy schedule to focus on God. God thinks having a Sabbath is so important for us that he made sure it made the list of ten commandments in Exodus 20.

Taking time for God is on the same list of commands as not murdering people.

Jesus even woke up early and found quiet places to pray away from everyone because he knew the importance of having a strong prayer life. If Jesus can take time away from his schedule of healing people and dying for our sins, you can take some time in your schedule each day to be with God.

You likely know how important it is to stay in shape physically. Eat healthily, work out, and do what you must to be fit. Hopefully, you know the importance of staying in "mental shape," too. Reading, learning, and always being mindful of your mental health are significant. More important than your physical and mental health is your spiritual health.

How fit are you spiritually? Have you been "benching the same weight" since you first became a Christian, or are you regularly growing? Are you running on empty because it's been too long since you've taken in some inspiration, or do you have a regular diet of it?

Devotional life habits are incredibly important to create, and there is no better time to make a habit than today!

REFLECTION QUESTIONS:

What does having a Sabbath mean to you? What are things you can or not do on your Sabbath to help you experience God?

____
____
____
____
____
____
____
____

When is the best time of day for you to spend time with God? Is your life better when you pray regularly, do devotions, or read the Bible? If yes, how so?

____
____
____
____
____
____
____
____

PRAYER:

God, I want to take this moment and just breathe and be in your presence. Thank you for being here with me. Please rejuvenate me so that I can better share you with others and live my best possible life. Thank you, Holy Spirit, for moving through the Bible, my prayer time, this devotional, and all the other ways you speak to me. Amen!

WEEK 9: SERVANT LEADERSHIP

Reading Plan for NIV Scriptures:

DAY 1: MATTHEW 20:25-28 *(To be great you must serve)*

DAY 2: JOHN 13:12-17 *(No servant is greater than his master)*

DAY 3: EPHESIANS 5:1-2 *(Follow Christ's example)*

DAY 4: LUKE 22:24-26 *(Christ calls a different kind of leader)*

DAY 5: PHILIPPIANS 2:3-4 *(Put others before you)*

DAY 6: MATTHEW 23:8-11 *(God is our only leader)*

DAY 7: 2 TIMOTHY 2:24 *(Be kind to everyone)*

WEEKLY COMMENTARY:

I was in a Christian band with friends from my youth group in high school. During my sophomore year, the guys who were our leaders graduated, and new leaders needed to be named. I wanted to be the leader of this band. I knew I would do a good job, and to be honest, I wanted the title of "Leader of the band."

Another guy my age wanted the same role, probably for the same reasons. The youth pastor finally sat down with us and stated that the other guy, not me, would be the leader. I was angry about it, but the youth pastor told me that just because I wasn't "in charge" didn't mean I wasn't a leader. How I followed the new leader would set an example for the younger students in the band. I quickly saw how correct he was because I noticed everyone looking at me whenever the leader made a decision. How I reacted would set the stage for how they reacted.

I ended up being a great leader, by how I was being a follower.

As Christians, we are called to follow Jesus's example in everything that we do. Jesus was certainly a leader, but not in the ways many people expected. The people of Jesus's time wanted a king on a majestic white horse. Jesus rode a donkey. They wanted a great leader who would command over everyone. Jesus washed his disciples' feet. The Jewish people in Jesus's day wanted a king to take them to the top. Jesus taught that the last shall be first.

If you want to lead like Jesus, then you need to learn how to lead by loving others and putting their needs before your own. It may not be as glamorous as the leaders we see on TV, but it's more effective and the way of our Lord and Savior, Jesus Christ.

Every single one of us is a leader. People look at you and follow your example, whether you like it or not, even if you're unaware of it. You don't get the choice of whether or not you are going to lead. What you get to choose is this:

1. What kind of leader are you going to be?

2. Are you going to be good at it or not?

I pray you follow Jesus's example and lead others by loving them and putting their needs before yours. By doing this, you will do more for them than their favorite revered celebrity ever could.

REFLECTION QUESTIONS:

What makes Jesus a good leader? Are there ways you can implement these qualities in your own life?

____
____
____
____
____
____
____
____

Who is it in your life that you can be a leader to? Who do you influence, and who would you like to influence?

____
____
____
____
____
____
____
____

PRAYER:

Thank you, Lord, for the example I find in Jesus Christ. Please help me look at Christ's example every day to lead me to be a better Christian in everything I do. Also, please help me lead like Christ does by putting others before me. Direct me to someone this week that I can lead into a relationship with You. Amen.

WEEK 10: DON'T COMPLAIN

Reading Plan for NIV Scriptures:

DAY 1:  PHILIPPIANS 2:14-16 *(Do everything without complaining)*

DAY 2: JAMES 5:9 *(Don't complain to each other)*

DAY 3: 1 PETER 4:9 *(Offer hospitality without complaining)*

DAY 4: 1 TIMOTHY 2:8 *(Pray instead of disputing)*

DAY 5: JOB 1:22 *(Don't complain even when things are terrible)*

DAY 6: JOHN 6:43 *(Don't complain)*

DAY 7: NUMBERS 11:1-2 *(Pray instead of complaining)*

WEEKLY COMMENTARY:

One of the hardest conversations I ever had to have with a friend was when he noticed we hadn't talked in a while and called to ask why. "Well, do you want to know the real reason?" I asked him. When he said yes, I told him. "You're always complaining, grumbling, or whining about something. Conversations with you are very emotionally draining, and I only have so much energy, so I just chose to have less of those conversations because they're not very life-giving."

I didn't feel bad telling him this because someone else had a similar conversation with me years prior. There is a difference between venting about current problems or asking for prayer in tough situations and being a chronic complainer. Some folks stew in their issues and negativity and don't know how to have conversations without complaining. It's very exhausting.

As Christians, we are called to be lights in the lives of our friends, family, and everyone we come into contact with. Conversations with us shouldn't feel like we're sapping the charge out of someone's battery. As a Christian, you should strive to have as little complaining and grumbling in your conversation as possible.

Why shouldn't we complain? Because it's among one of the most useless things, you can use words for. Typically a complaint is centered around an issue that you have no control over. There is a difference between raising awareness on something that can change and just grumbling about whatever you are unhappy with. One leads to a change in circumstance, and another is just a waste of words that leaves people in a less good mood.

Your words have power, but when you complain, you can quickly diminish the value of what you say to others. As a Christian, I strive to have the kind of conversations with others that they would consider life-giving and positive. Try to help everyone feel a little better after a conversation with you.

This week, think about the topics you typically discuss with your friends. Are you all better off because of your conversations, or are you all wasting each other's time and energy?

REFLECTION QUESTIONS:

How often do you complain? What are the things that you are most tempted to grumble about?

____

____

____

____

____

____

____

____

How can you strive to be more positive this week with your words and conversations?

____

____

____

____

____

____

____

____

PRAYER:

Lord, please help me be content in all circumstances, even the hardest ones. Holy Spirit, please help control my tongue so that when I am tempted to grumble, You help me not to. Please put the people in my life to encourage this conversation style and help me be a light to them. Amen.

WEEK 11: HONORING YOUR PARENTS

Reading Plan for NIV Scriptures:

DAY 1: EXODUS 20:12 *(Honor your father and mother)*

DAY 2: 1 PETER 2:13-17 *(Respect Authority)*

DAY 3: PROVERBS 10:17 *(Discipline can bring growth)*

DAY 4: PROVERBS 15:5 *(Fools don't listen to their parents)*

DAY 5: PROVERBS 23:13 *(Discipline comes from God)*

DAY 6: PROVERBS 17:6 *(Parents are blessings)*

DAY 7: EPHESIANS 6:1-3 *(Obey your parents to have a better life)*

WEEKLY COMMENTARY:

One of my favorite older rappers is Will Smith. That's right, *"kids"* before Will Smith was a movie star, he was making big moves as a rapper in the 90s. One of my favorite Will Smith songs is titled "Parents Just Don't Understand."

Can you relate to your parents not understanding you at some point? I think every human on earth can. That's why the song was such a hit.

In the Bible, God tells us to honor our mom and dad. It made it to his Top Ten (the 10 Commandments). That's right; God thought honoring our parents was enough of a rule that he put it on the same list as "Don't murder." That should let you know how important it is to God that we respect our parents.

There are many ways we can honor our parents. Listening to them, respecting their authority, and being nice at home, are all ways you've probably thought of and hopefully do. Did you know you can honor your parents through the life you live? You are their legacy, so you are honoring your parents by being successful and pleasing to God with your life.

You have probably been told before to respect and honor your parents, but have you ever considered that God put you in your family so that He could work through you to witness to them?

That's right; you can share Jesus with your family by being a good Christian example in everything you do at home. Our families are the hardest to minister to because they know us the best...for better or worse. They have seen you when you are most annoying and love you anyway.

When you are patient with your parents, when you respect them, when you are kind, or even if you respectfully disagree, these are all ways you can be a light for Jesus in their lives.

As you interact with your parents this week, think about how you can be a good Christian role model to them. Even adults need good role models!

REFLECTION QUESTIONS:

How can you honor your parents and share God with them this week?

____

____

____

____

____

____

____

____

What are you most grateful for regarding your parents? What is your favorite part of them? (As an added challenge and opportunity, you should share this answer with your parents at some point this week!)

____

____

____

____

____

____

____

____

PRAYER:

God, thank you for my parents. Thank you for providing for me through them. I pray that you bless my steps, actions, and words so that I live in a way that honors and respects them. Please give me self-control for the times that they frustrate me and help me act in a way that isn't disrespectful. Help me spot ways that I can be a positive influence on my parents. Amen

WEEK 12: BEING A GODLY BROTHER

Reading Plan for NIV Scriptures:

DAY 1: 📖 HEBREWS 10:24-25 *(Spur others on to good deeds)*

DAY 2: 📖 1 TIMOTHY 5:8 *(Provide for your relatives)*

DAY 3: 📖 JAMES 4:11 *(Don't slander each other)*

DAY 4: 📖 JOHN 1:41 *(Share Jesus with your siblings)*

DAY 5: 📖 PSALM 133:1 *(It's good to live in unity)*

DAY 6: 📖 1 JOHN 4:20-21 *(It's ungodly to love others but not your family)*

DAY 7: 📖 1 JOHN 3:12 *(Don't be jealous of your siblings)*

WEEKLY COMMENTARY:

I am the youngest in my family, and when I was a child, I worshiped the ground my older brother walked on. Everything he did, I wanted to do. Wherever he was, I wanted to be. If he had an opinion on an issue, it became my opinion. I followed him everywhere...and I can't imagine how annoying it was for him as a slightly older child!

I got used to statements like, "Go away!" or doors slamming in my face or occasionally being thrown out of his room. Once, he even tied me to a chair and left me in a closet. When my mom figured this out, I think she almost murdered my brother. I annoyed my older brother just as much as I worshiped him. Looking back, I bothered him on purpose sometimes just because it was so fun and so easy.

Relationships with our siblings is one of the unique kinds of relationships that exist. You didn't choose your family, but they are with you for your whole life. They know you, for better or for worse. Your family has seen you at your best and will see you at your worst. You know all the gory details of each of your siblings and your parents, and hopefully, you love them regardless.

One of the unique things about family is that these are the people that we will likely be spending the most time with, especially when you're a teenager and living at home with them. So if you're a brother, whether an older one or younger, you have a very special relationship with someone else that God wants to use to improve their life.

Your family is where you can share Jesus the most. How you act when nobody's looking and the kind of person you are at home are ways that they can see good Christian character in a setting where they aren't expecting it, making it more impactful.

You can share Jesus by the way you treat your siblings. By being a good listener or by giving them their space. By sharing advice or modeling a good life. By standing up or being present during times of trouble.

God has placed you and your siblings together on purpose, so don't forget to share Jesus by the kind of brother you are.

REFLECTION QUESTIONS:

What is the relationship with your sibling (or siblings) like? What are your favorite and least favorite parts of them?

____

____

____

____

____

____

____

How can you share Jesus this week with your sibling (or siblings)? What practical ways can you be a good Christian role model for your family?

____

____

____

____

____

____

____

PRAYER:

God, thank you for giving me the gift of my family. I pray this week that I am able to be a good Christian witness in the way I live and the words I say at home. If there are any times I am irritable or annoying with my siblings or parents, please give me the patience to be able to continue to share You well with them. Amen.

WEEK 13: CONSIDER YOUR SOURCE

Reading Plan for NIV Scriptures:

DAY 1: PSALM 118:6-9 *(The Lord is with you)*

DAY 2: 1 THESSALONIANS 2:4 *(Please God, not people)*

DAY 3: 2 TIMOTHY 2:15 *(Do your best for God's approval)*

DAY 4: 2 CORINTHIANS 10:18 *(The Lord, not us, does the commending)*

DAY 5: MATTHEW 6:1 *(Don't work for other people's approval)*

DAY 6: JOHN 6:27 *(God's rewards last forever)*

DAY 7: PROVERBS 29:25 *(It is safe to trust the Lord)*

WEEKLY COMMENTARY:

Whenever I used to get made fun of in school when I was younger, I would go home and tell my mom all about it. I would be very upset and would recite all the names people called me and all the rude things the kids would say. My mom would always respond the same, "Who said that to you?" When I told her, she'd give the same retort, "Well...consider your sources."

That was her way of saying, "That kid's opinion of you really doesn't matter. What they are saying isn't important." It didn't always make me feel 100% better, but it was nice to hear my mom tell me that the bullies in my school, or at least the things they said, really didn't matter.

Today I want to challenge you with the same words, "Consider your source." We spend so much time seeking the approval of others. What do my friends think of me? What does my family think of me? What do the cool kids in school think of me? What does my teacher think of me?

Statistically, this is most common with middle schoolers. Did you know by the time you're in around 6th grade, is when you *first* become aware of the question, "What do others think of me?" Before then, you're only able to process what you think of things. By the time we hit middle and high school, we have a new concern biologically...what others think.

People, especially teenagers, stress the opinions and approval of those around them so much. Ultimately, this is a useless exercise because everyone, even your favorite person on earth, is flawed. Suppose you define everything about yourself based on the opinions of one person. Eventually, that person will let you down, or you will let them down.

Instead, putting all your time and effort into seeking God's approval is much better. First, God approves you every day, no matter who you are. Secondly, by living a life that you know God is proud of, you can become the best version of yourself in a way that will make life better for you and everyone around you. Third, and most importantly, God's standards are much better than anyone else's, so when you strive for God's approval, you are always in the right.

If people don't like the life you live, but God does, then you are living life correctly.

REFLECTION QUESTIONS:

Apart from God, who are the people in your life whose approval you seek the most, and why? When is this a good thing, and when can it be bad?

____
____
____
____
____
____
____
____

What are examples of ways that you can live that you know God approves of? How is your life better when living for God and not other people?

____
____
____
____
____
____
____
____

PRAYER:

God, you are my master, ruler, and greatest authority. I give you everything that I am and ask that you continue to mold me to be the best version of myself every day. Thank you for always loving me, even when I mess up. I pray that you help me live a life you approve of today and every single day! Amen.

WEEK 14: THE HOLY SPIRIT

Reading Plan for NIV Scriptures:

DAY 1: 📖 JOHN 14:25-27 *(The Holy Spirit is our advocate)*

DAY 2: 📖 ROMANS 8:5-9 *(The Spirit sets our mind on what God desires)*

DAY 3: 📖 1 CORINTHIANS 12:4-11 *(The Holy Spirit gives spiritual gifts)*

DAY 4: 📖 MICAH 3:8 *(The Holy Spirit empowers us)*

DAY 5: 📖 ACTS 13:2 *(The Holy Spirit calls us)*

DAY 6: 📖 PSALM 143:10 *(The Holy Spirit teaches us)*

DAY 7: 📖 ACTS 2:38 *(The Holy Spirit is a gift)*

WEEKLY COMMENTARY:

Several years ago, I worked at a grocery store, and part of my job was to train all the new employees and show them around the store. One of the parts of the job that I enjoyed the most was when I was able to tell them all the benefits they received from working this job. I made sure they knew about the health benefits and the discounts they would get with certain cell phone providers. I also made sure they knew about the discounts in the surrounding stores they could get just by bringing their name tag from the grocery store. And, of course, I never forgot to tell them about Burrito Monday at the Mexican restaurant across the street because that was one of the best parts of the week.

I remember thinking, "If you're going to work here, why would you not want to know about all the benefits you receive?"

When you became a Christian, you gave your life to Jesus, and he took your place on the cross and saved you from your sins. But that's not all. When you give your life to Jesus, he also gives you the best gift that you have ever received. The Holy Spirit.

The Holy Spirit is one of the greatest benefits of living a life pursuing God, and it's one that is not talked about nearly enough.

The Holy Spirit directs you. It strengthens you. It gives you gifts and counsel. It comforts and creates passion in you as God directs your path. It will give you the words to say when you think you have nothing to say, and it will guide you to not speak in times when you should say nothing. Most importantly, the Holy Spirit works in your heart to transform you into the best version of yourself as God intended.

Along with God the Father and Jesus Christ, the Holy Spirit is part of the Holy Trinity. That same Spirit is with you everywhere you go and works daily.

Wow! Take a moment and let that soak in.

The Holy Spirit is the closest to a superpower we will ever have. God's power is inside of you. God's voice, inside of you. God's direction, guiding you. Any time you feel overwhelmed, remember you are not alone. The Holy Spirit is right here with you, every moment of every day.

What a gift! I hope you enjoy this amazing gift God has graciously given us all.

REFLECTION QUESTIONS:

What is your relationship and experience with the Holy Spirit? Have you ever felt its presence? Has the Holy Spirit ever directed you in a way that you knew it was God without a doubt?

____
____
____
____
____
____
____
____

What is one thing this week that you'd like to ask for from the Holy Spirit?

____
____
____
____
____
____
____
____

PRAYER:

Thank you, Jesus, for the gift of the Holy Spirit! Holy Spirit, please continue to guide me and transform me to be more like the best version of myself, as God intends. Direct me every day, and give me the strength and bravery to follow you. Amen.

WEEK 15: YOUR WILL BE DONE

Reading Plan for NIV Scriptures:

DAY 1: 📖 MICAH 6:8 *(Act justly, love mercy, and walk humbly with God)*

DAY 2: 📖 PHILIPPIANS 4:4-9 *(Pray to God about everything)*

DAY 3: 📖 MATTHEW 6:33-34 *(Seek God's Kingdom First)*

DAY 4: 📖 JEREMIAH 29:11-13 *(God has plans for you)*

DAY 5: 📖 JOHN 14:23-24 *(We love God by obeying Him)*

DAY 6: 📖 COLOSSIANS 3:1-3 *(Set your minds on things above)*

DAY 7: 📖 PSALM 119:105-112 *(God's word directs you)*

WEEKLY COMMENTARY:

For years I have played the keyboard, and I always love it when I get a new keyboard. I am usually up all night playing around with the new instrument, experimenting with all the sounds, pressing all the buttons, and exploring my new device. It's very exciting, but on my own, I am never able to discover everything that the instrument has to offer.

Thank goodness for owners manuals. Someone who had a hand in building the device took the time and effort to write out everything that the keyboard has to offer. When I read the owner's manual, I discover not just the surface-level functions that I could figure out alone but I learn the more complex functions that require pushing more than one button.

It makes sense that the creator would know more about how to work their creation than I would. In the same way, your Creator knows everything about you and all the amazing things you can do.

As Christians, we often pray, "Your will be done," and we are encouraged to live not by our own standards but by God's. Surely if you've been going to church for any amount of time, at least once, someone has told you the importance of "God's plan for you" or asked you, "What does God want you to do with your life?"

We even ask, "Have you surrendered your life to Christ?"

The thing about God's will for you is that it's better than any plan you could make for yourself. God knows the best possible version of you and everything else about everyone else in this world. God knows how you can live your best life and how that life can change this world for the better.

I hope with all my heart that you give your life, plans, dreams, and every step you take to God. I hope you get into the habit of following Him wholeheartedly and constantly seeking His will over your own.

REFLECTION QUESTIONS:

What are the plans, goals, dreams, and aspirations you have for yourself? What are the steps you are taking to make these dreams realities?

____
____
____
____
____
____
____
____

What is God's will for you? What does God want you to do with your life? If you haven't ever asked yourself this question, take some time this week and reflect on it. Use the space provided to share what you think God wants for you personally.

____
____
____
____
____
____
____
____

PRAYER:

Lord, I ask that it's not my will, but your will be done. Please guide me in every one of my steps, and make your ways known to me. I submit my wants, goals, plans, and dreams to you and am ready to listen and be obedient to the direction that you take me. It might be scary, but I know you will be with me every step of the way. Thank you, Jesus. Amen.

WEEK 16: ACTIONS SPEAK LOUDER THAN WORDS

Reading Plan for NIV Scriptures:

DAY 1: JAMES 1:22-25 (*Don't just listen to the Word, do it*)

DAY 2: EPHESIANS 5:6-7 (*Don't say it if you don't do it*)

DAY 3: JAMES 2:14-17 (*Faith is followed by Action*)

DAY 4: MATTHEW 5:33-37 (*Keep your word*)

DAY 5: 1 JOHN 3:18 (*Actions speak louder than words*)

DAY 6: TITUS 1:10-18 (*Claiming God's word but not living it is detestable*)

DAY 7: PSALM 119:1-3 (*God blesses those who follow His ways*)

WEEKLY COMMENTARY:

What do you think the biggest critique of Christianity is?

Have you ever spoken to someone who isn't a fan of Christianity or Christians? If so, have you ever asked them why they feel that way? In my experience, many people who have issues with Christianity have little to no problem with God but with His followers. The biggest criticism we get as Christians is that our people are *Hypocrites*.

A hypocrite is someone who says one thing and does something that is contrary to what they say. So a Christian is a hypocrite could be someone who shares how their God is all about love, but then that person treats people poorly.

I remember the first Christians I ever met. I had moved to a new school, and the same group of guys that were taking me to the bathroom to knock me around were passing out flyers at lunch for the Christian group that met once a week before school started. I can't tell you how meaningless it was to hear "Jesus loves you" from a guy that stuck my head in a toilet a few hours beforehand. I never went to their club.

Contrast that to the people I met the first time I ever went to church a year or so later. They found me after the church service, introduced themselves to me, and invited me to their Sunday school class the next week. When I showed up the next week, they remembered my name and invited me to sit with them. The teacher taught us about how Jesus loves everyone and so should we, and I was impressed with the model I saw from the Christians in that class.

I hope you tell people about God with your words. I hope you share Bible verses and pray for others when you can. More importantly, I hope your actions back up your faith. The reality is your actions can either help or hurt your words. If you are preaching Christ but not living a good Christian life, you are not doing God any favors; you might be pushing people away from God.

The good news is that it is never too late to start living a holy life that points people to God in addition to the words you share about Him! Think about your actions this week as a Christian. Do they represent your faith well? If you suddenly couldn't speak tomorrow, would people be able to tell you are a Christian by how you live your life?

REFLECTION QUESTIONS:

Who is someone you feel is a very good Christian who lives a holy life that impresses you? What is it about their faith and lifestyle that impresses you?

How do you share Jesus with how you live your life and treat others?

PRAYER:

God, I pray for opportunities to share you with everyone I come in contact with. Give me the words to speak when necessary, but please move through the way I live my life and how I treat others. Please give me extra patience when I interact with people that annoy me and help me love someone this week that is hard to love and really needs it. Let my actions preach about you as loudly, if not louder than my words! Amen.

WEEK 17: THE COMPANY WE KEEP

Reading Plan for NIV Scriptures:

DAY 1: 2 TIMOTHY 3:1-5 *(Have nothing to do with ungodly people)*

DAY 2: GALATIANS 6:1-2 *(Don't fall in someone else's sin)*

DAY 3: PROVERBS 18:24 *(Don't have unreliable friends)*

DAY 4: PROVERBS 14:7 *(Stay away from a fool)*

DAY 5: PSALM 1:1 *(Blessed is one who doesn't walk with the wicked)*

DAY 6: PSALM 119:115 *(Avoid people keeping you from God's commands)*

DAY 7: PSALM 26:4-5 *(Refuse to be with evildoers)*

WEEKLY COMMENTARY:

When I was a freshman in college, I had to make a completely new group of friends because I moved far away from the friends I had in high school. I remember that I started to hang out with a group of girls that were nice enough, but they were highly dramatic and frequently spoke poorly about others and gossiped a lot. This wasn't the behavior I was used to from my old friend group, but they were the first people I met, and they accepted me, so I became good friends with them.

When I was home for Christmas break, I realized that I had developed some pretty bad habits. It was easier for me to gravitate towards "Drama," and I was becoming a bit of a gossip myself. When one of my friends from back home pointed this out, I realized that the new company I was keeping had started to influence how I was acting.

You've heard the phrase, "You are what you eat," but did you know there is another phrase that is just as true...You are who you hang out with.

Who we spend our time with will shape how we talk, what we're interested in, and, eventually, how we think. A good friend can help you grow into a better person, and a bad friend can bring you down. Unfortunately, it's easier to be brought down than it is to bring someone up. Suppose your whole friend group is full of negativity and mean behavior. In that case, it'll be easier for you to start slumming it in their behavior than to elevate them all to more Christlike actions.

Jesus calls us to love everyone and build relationships with those that are far from him, but we shouldn't have the kind of relationships where we are shaped to be less like Jesus because of the people in our lives. A friend of mine says, "Be friendly to everyone, but choose your friends wisely."

In the same way, what kind of company do YOU generate? Are you a positive and encouraging friend that helps elevate people to higher standards? Or are you a friend who brings people down because of their language, behavior, or lifestyle? Strive to always add something positive to each relationship you are part of.

When I returned to college my freshman year after Christmas, I found a better group of best friends I would hang out with regularly. We went to church together, we had Bible studies in the dorm, and they helped me grow into a better person. I stayed friends with the first group I met during my first semester; they weren't my best friends. And that's okay!

REFLECTION QUESTIONS:

Who are your best friends, favorite people, and those you spend the most time with? How do they make your life better?

____
____
____
____
____
____
____

What do you bring to your friend circles, church, and family to add to other people's lives? In other words, what could be the "perks" of being in a friendship with you?

____
____
____
____
____
____
____
____

PRAYER:

God, help me worship you by monitoring the people I choose to give significant roles in my life. Help me find wonderful and encouraging friends that you can shine through to enhance my life. Also, help me live in a kind of way where I share You with others by being the best possible friend I can be. Amen.

WEEK 18: BULLIES

Reading Plan for NIV Scriptures:

DAY 1: 📖 ROMANS 12:17-21 *(Do not repay evil with evil)*

DAY 2: 📖 MATTHEW 5:43-48 *(Love your enemies)*

DAY 3: 📖 LUKE 6:27-31 *(Do good to those who hate you)*

DAY 4: 📖 GALATIANS 6:7-8 *(A man reaps what they sow)*

DAY 5: 📖 2 TIMOTHY 1:7-9 *(The Spirit of God gives us power)*

DAY 6: 📖 DEUTERONOMY 31:6 *(Do not be afraid because God is with you)*

DAY 7: 📖 MATTHEW 5:10-12 *(We are blessed when we are persecuted)*

WEEKLY COMMENTARY:

Bullies were the hardest part of my middle and high school years. In addition to those kids saying or doing mean and hateful things, I always had a hard time with the "Christian response" to bullies. Any time I asked for prayer about a circumstance, someone would always want to add in, "And let's pray for the bully too." Or whenever I'd look up scripture on how to deal with the bullies, I'd find verses that say things like "Turn the other cheek" or "vengeance is for the Lord."

I was always hoping for permission from God to knock my bullies out, but I never was given that kind of freedom. Here's what I know:

We can't control the actions of others; we can only control our own actions. Never let a jerk or bully dictate how you act because you respond to their unkindness with your own. God calls us to be lights and better than the jerks. When you repay evil with evil, you lose just as much as the other person, and it's never as fulfilling as you're hoping for.

Also, there isn't a bully that exists or who has ever existed that God doesn't love and see the incredible value and worth in. They may not be living their best life, but God knows what their best life is and wants it for them. We love God by loving who God loves, and as much as you might hate to hear it...God loves your bully.

Please understand that not repaying evil with evil doesn't mean "just let evil happen." God also calls us to protect those in need; sometimes, we are in need. If you can stop the bullying, tell an adult, or find ways to provide for someone who is being bullied, these are all examples of sharing Christian love with others. There is a difference between stopping a fight, picking up a crowbar, and smashing someone's lights out because they have hurt you. One is a Christian response, and the other most definitely is not.

If you are being bullied, please know that everything works out in the end through God. I am sorry this is happening to you, but it is temporary. God will provide for you, and the bully will "reap what he/she sows," as the Bible says. Keep strong, do the right thing, and God will move you to better circumstances!

REFLECTION QUESTIONS:

How do you think God views a bully? How does God feel about him/her? What does God think about how they are living? How do you think God will handle them?

____
____
____
____
____
____
____

As a Christian, what can you do when you're being bullied? What can you do when someone else is being bullied? How can you be a witness to the bully?

____
____
____
____
____
____
____

PRAYER:

Lord, I want to lift up all the bullies, my own included. Please deliver them from any harsh conditions that lead them to act the way they are currently acting. Please transform their hearts in a way that changes the way they behave and the decisions they make. Lord, please change my heart too to help me better love the bullies and see them the way that you see them. Amen.

WEEK 19: FORGIVING OTHERS

Reading Plan for NIV Scriptures:

DAY 1: EPHESIANS 4:30-32 *(Forgive others as Christ forgave you)*

DAY 2: COLOSSIANS 3:12-14 *(Forgive one another)*

DAY 3: MATTHEW 6:12-15 *(Pray for those you need to forgive)*

DAY 4: LUKE 6:37-38 *(Forgive so you can be forgiven)*

DAY 5: MATTHEW 18:21-35 *(We need forgiveness)*

DAY 6: PROVERBS 17:9 *(Love covers offenses)*

DAY 7: PROVERBS 10:12 *(Love can silence conflicts)*

WEEKLY COMMENTARY:

If you could only pick one accomplishment, what do you think Jesus would be remembered for the most?

Jesus certainly had a full thirty-three years on earth, and he did a lot of memorable things. Living a perfect life. All those miracles. His great teachings. But what would be his one "Claim to fame"?It would have to be when He died on the cross for all of us through the power of God and forgave all of humanity for our sins. As wonderful as everything else about Jesus is, that's his greatest feat.

Jesus and forgiveness are closely connected. This means that when we have the opportunity to forgive others, we have the opportunity to shine the most Christ-like characteristic that exists. You are most like Jesus when you forgive someone, especially for something you deem unforgivable!

The Bible is also very clear on God's expectation on forgiveness. Christ commands us to do it and even goes as far as saying if we don't forgive, then we are not forgiven. I believe this doesn't mean that God can't forgive us if we are unable to forgive someone. We must ask for God's forgiveness, and many times when we are so bitter and unable to forgive someone else, we are less likely to ask God to forgive us.

Forgiveness should be a very active part of your life. You should be in the habit of forgiving others, which liberates you more than that person. You should also be in the habit of going to God for forgiveness. When we are comfortable accepting forgiveness for our sins, forgiving others is easier.

God changed the world with forgiveness; think about the impact you can make on others if you are able to forgive them. Furthermore, the best part about forgiving others is letting go of the pain they caused that is binding you down. Forgiveness allows you to take power back from those that have hurt you.

REFLECTION QUESTIONS:

What impact can forgiving others for "the unforgivable" have on those people? What kind of impact can it have on you?

____
____
____
____
____
____
____

Take a hard look at your life and relationships currently. Is there anyone that you feel God is calling you to forgive?

____
____
____
____
____
____
____

PRAYER:

Help me, Lord, take a long hard look at all my relationships this week and consider who it is in my life that you are calling me to forgive. Please heal my heart and give me the strength to be able to forgive this person or these people. Thank you for always being ready to forgive me, and I pray that I never lose sight of your wonderful love for your children, myself included. Amen!

WEEK 20: LIFE WITHOUT FILTERS

Reading Plan for NIV Scriptures:

DAY 1: 1 PETER 3:3-4 *(Your beauty comes from inside)*

DAY 2: 1 JOHN 2:15-17 *(Worldly desires pass away)*

DAY 3: PSALM 139:14-16 *(You are wonderfully made)*

DAY 4: ACTS 1:8 *(The Holy Spirit empowers you)*

DAY 5: PROVERBS 16:3 *(The Lord will establish your plans)*

DAY 6: JEREMIAH 1:5 *(God formed you in the womb)*

DAY 7: 2 THESSALONIANS 1:11-12 *(Jesus Christ is glorified through you)*

WEEKLY COMMENTARY:

Thanks to social media, we live in an age of filters. There is so much pressure when we post pictures on Facebook, Instagram, Snapchat, or whatever social media is currently in at the time of you reading this devotional to make sure everything looks "perfect." Is the lighting good? Does your skin look tan enough? How white are your teeth? How are the angles of the picture?

And then there is the caption. However you word your post, you want to make sure everyone reading thinks you have an absolutely *perfect* life. Filter out any insecurities any problems, and make sure you sound like you're having the best time ever and whoever isn't in this picture or post is missing out.

We put so much pressure on ourselves when posting for others to see. The message behind this pressure is simple. *We don't think we're good enough to post without filters.*

But please read these words and let your heart hear them: *God didn't make you with a filter. God made you as is, and that is more than good enough!*

The Bible calls us God's workmanship and tells us that God knitted us together in our mother's womb. We are fearful and wonderfully made. You don't need to filter your pictures, personality, or thoughts because you are made on purpose and awesome as is. In a world that is always telling people, "you aren't good enough as is," the Bible reminds us that we are MORE THAN good enough as is.

People crave what is real. We want authentic relationships with authentic people. The real you is better than the filtered you every time. It's scary sometimes to be real when it's so easy to be fake, but I promise it is always worth it, not just for you but everyone else that is blessed to have the real version of you in their life.

Don't settle for a filtered version of yourself both on social media and in real life. Don't cheap people out of the real you. God made you intentionally with purpose as is. This week go out of your way to be authentic.

REFLECTION QUESTIONS:

What are some of the things you are most insecure about yourself? How could God shine through those exact same traits?

____
____
____
____
____
____
____

What does it mean to you that you are made in God's image, you are considered a masterpiece by Him, and that you are fearfully and wonderfully made? Does this change the way you view yourself?

____
____
____
____
____
____
____

PRAYER:

God, thank you so much for making me so intentional and loving every part of me. Thank you for the parts that I am proud of in myself, and I pray that you help me love the parts of me that I am not yet a huge fan of. God, help me see others the way you see them, and also help me see Myself the way you do. Amen.

WEEK 21: LISTEN!

Reading Plan for NIV Scriptures:

DAY 1: 📖 PSALM 119:9-16 *(Listen to God to stay pure)*

DAY 2: 📖 2 TIMOTHY 3:16-17 *(Listen to God through scripture)*

DAY 3: 📖 JOHN 10:27-28 *(Listening to God will protect you)*

DAY 4: 📖 PROVERBS 2:1-5 *(Listening to God leads to wisdom)*

DAY 5: 📖 PSALM 25:4-5 *(Listening to God leads you down the best path)*

DAY 6: 📖 ROMANS 10:17 *(Listening to God develops faith)*

DAY 7: 📖 JAMES 1:19 *(Be quick to listen and slow to speak)*

WEEKLY COMMENTARY:

When I was a kid, I played this video game called Legend of Zelda, Ocarina of Time on the Nintendo 64 (I know, I'm ancient). In this game, this annoying little blue fairy would constantly yell at you, "Listen!" until you stopped what you were doing and chose to listen to her. When you did, she would give you tips about the game or useful information about the next part. I don't think I could have made it through the game if I had never stopped to listen to Navi the fairy.

We don't have a little blue fairy constantly bugging us to listen. Still, we have an all-power and loving God who knows everything about us and all of our existence and wants to have a relationship with each and every one of us. That includes you.

When was the last time you *listened* to God? Notice I didn't ask. When was the last time you prayed to Him? Often our prayers are all very one-sided. It often is just us talking to God. Giving him a list of requests, followed by us venting about our problems, and ending with us saying, "Thank you and Amen!"

Can you imagine if you had a friend that spoke to you the way we speak to God? Always talking and never letting you get a word in.

Listening to God can be so beneficial. God can direct your steps. He can give you peace. He can help you understand the world and all the people you interact with. He can comfort you. God has a lot to share with you if you take the opportunity to quiet down and let Him.

God speaks to us in many different ways, and it's important to realize it probably won't be a loud audible voice from a burning bush like it was with Moses. God speaks in prayer and in our hearts. God speaks through scripture. God speaks through nature. God speaks through other people. God speaks in sermons and other forms of media. God speaks; however, God wants to speak because God can do whatever He wants. It's up to us to be willing to listen and learn how we hear God the best.

This week make a point to listen to God as much, if not maybe a little more than you speak to Him. I bet He'll share with you something that is spectacular!

REFLECTION QUESTIONS:

Where do you find you hear God the best? Do you have a specific location, time of day, or method? (Some, but not all, the ways we can hear God include prayer, scripture, worship music, sermons, community, silence, media, and nature)

____
____
____
____
____
____
____

Take some time every day to be silent and listen to God. Give yourself one to five minutes of pure silence, and just listen to God. What is He sharing with you?

____
____
____
____
____
____
____

PRAYER:

Thank you, God, for the gift of prayer and the ability to come to you anytime and anywhere, no matter what is going on. During my prayer time today, I would like to shut my mouth and open my ears, and hear your voice. Please take this time to share with me what you'd like me to hear. Amen.

(Give yourself some time of silence and let the Holy Spirit move)

WEEK 22: WORSHIP

Reading Plan for NIV Scriptures:

DAY 1: ROMANS 12:1-2 *(We are living sacrifices to God)*

DAY 2: PSALM 136:1-3 *(Giving thanks to God is worship)*

DAY 3: PSALM 103:1-2 *(Praise God with everything you are)*

DAY 4: 1 CHRONICLES 16:8-12 *(Worship God by remembering His works)*

DAY 5: PSALM 95:6-7 *(Submitting to God is worship)*

DAY 6: HEBREWS 12:28-29 *(God is worthy of our awe and reverence)*

DAY 7: EXODUS 20:3 *(We shall only worship God)*

WEEKLY COMMENTARY:

The word *worship* literally means "Worth-Ship," as in the act of aspiring worth to something. By that definition, it is possible to "worth-ship" many things. We see the worth in our sports and extracurricular activities, which is why we spend hours practicing and training ourselves regardless of how uncomfortable and hard conditioning might be. We see worth in our family and friends, which is why we spend so much of our time caring for them, wanting to be around them, or maybe even buying things for them.

You may *give worth* to a lot of things, but you only *worship* God. Whatever it is that you aspire the most worth to, that is what you worship. God is worthy of all our worship and more, and only God is worthy of worship. God knows it, too; that's why He forbids us from worshiping anything else.

What we worship shapes us. You are possibly at the age where you might have a friend (or this may be you) who is obsessed with a girlfriend that they (or you) have just started dating. People say, "*He worships the ground she walks on.*" Typically it's not uncommon for people to change completely when they are around a girlfriend/boyfriend they are into with the hopes of being the most worthy of their partner.

This is a terrible way of dating someone, but it's not terrible for how we should worship God. Everything about us is a "living sacrifice" to God. How we live our lives, how we treat others, and how we think and pray can be fragrant offerings to the God we worship.

Are you giving God your best? Are you giving Him your mediocre? Are you giving Him your leftovers?

There is no one more majestic than God. There is no one more powerful than God. There is nobody that loves you more than God. There isn't a person you know, or one that has ever existed, who is more worthy of your worship than God.

Fully devote yourself to God in worship, and you will never be disappointed with the results.

REFLECTION QUESTIONS:

What are ways you aspire worth to God? *(This can be in how you spend your time, money, effort, energy, thoughts, or anything else)*

____
____
____
____
____
____
____

What is the best and most powerful worship experience you have ever had? What made it so special? Why do you think you experienced God so much at this moment?

____
____
____
____
____
____
____

PRAYER:

God, you are so worthy of my worship. I want to take this moment and appreciate how amazing and almighty you are. Thank you for providing for me and giving me space where I can personally have a conversation with you in prayer. Help me live my life in a way that I am a living sacrifice to you in everything that I do and in all the relationships I have. Amen.

WEEK 23: WORSHIPPING GOD THROUGH SCHOOL

Reading Plan for NIV Scriptures:

DAY 1: DEUTERONOMY 6:4-9 *(Love the Lord with your mind)*

DAY 2: COLOSSIANS 2:1-8 *(Don't be taken captive by deceptive teaching)*

DAY 3: PROVERBS 10:14 *(It is wise to gain knowledge)*

DAY 4: COLOSSIANS 3:23 *(Work for God in everything you do)*

DAY 5: PROVERBS 15:2 *(Wise people share knowledge)*

DAY 6: PROVERBS 18:15 *(Seek out knowledge)*

DAY 7: HOSEA 4:6 *(Lack of knowledge can lead to destruction)*

WEEKLY COMMENTARY:

Doing well in school can be an act of worship to God

I didn't learn this until I was almost done with my master's degree, and I really wish someone had told me sooner when I was in middle school or high school. Maybe someone tried. Knowing myself, I probably wasn't listening!

We should strive to give God the best in everything we do. You want to be the best person possible as an act of worship to God. You want to do your best in every sport and extracurricular activity to honor God with the gifts that He gave you. In the same way, you should strive to make the best grades possible and learn the most with the brain He gave you.

Learning is an amazing blessing that we should not take for granted. Education is one of the few things in this world that can only help people. Nobody has ever gotten hurt from learning too much! The book of Proverbs frequently states how the wise should want to amass as much knowledge as possible.

The answer to the question, *"When am I ever going to use this?"* is "I don't know… but now you have it in case you ever need it!"

Often the learning process is as educational as whatever topic we are learning. You should take it seriously and value it for its true gift. Acquiring knowledge also gives you something else you can share with others. The true point of education isn't solely so that *you learn* but so that you take what you learn and *teach it to others*. Regardless of what information you share, when you do it out of love, you also share Jesus with them.

The Bible says, "Love the Lord your God with all your heart, soul, mind, and strength." So let every test you take, every project you do, every book you read, and every assignment you complete be an opportunity to honor God with your mind.

REFLECTION QUESTIONS:

Think about your classes, going to school, and everything about the grade you are in right now. What are ways that you can worship God with your mind currently?

____

____

____

____

____

____

____

How can you share God with others at school? (In the class and outside of it)

____

____

____

____

____

____

____

PRAYER:

God, thank you for the gift of knowledge and for blessing me with a brain so that I may learn everything that you intend for me to know. Help me remember to honor you through my schoolwork in every test I take, the project I complete, an assignment I turn in, and a book I read. Give me the strength to work hard in the classes I don't excel in. Amen.

WEEK 24: INTEGRITY

Reading Plan for NIV Scriptures:

DAY 1: 📖 PROVERBS 10:9 *(Men of integrity walk securely)*

DAY 2: 📖 JAMES 5:12 *(Keep your word)*

DAY 3: 📖 1 PETER 2:12 *(Live faultlessly among others)*

DAY 4: 📖 1 TIMOTHY 4:12 *(Set an example by how you live)*

DAY 5: 📖 2 CORINTHIANS 8:21 *(Do what's right in the eyes of the Lord)*

DAY 6: 📖 ACTS 24:16 *(Strive to keep your conscious clear)*

DAY 7: 📖 HEBREWS 13:18 *(Try to live honorably in every way)*

WEEKLY COMMENTARY:

My grandfather was the best man that I ever knew. He was always kind, always honest, and strived to be the best man he could be every day. He was honorable, took pride in having good character, and encouraged his children and grandchildren to do the same.

The interesting thing is that even though my grandfather is the most impressive man I have ever met, you would not know about him at first glance. He wasn't highly athletic, and he didn't have a ton of money. He wasn't a vibrant speaker, nor did he have several degrees. His car was just average, and he was a very soft-spoken man.

What he had was integrity, and that's a virtue all men should have. You don't always have to be the smartest, best-looking, or richest person in the room. But you should pride yourself on trying your best to be the most honorable.

It is better to fail a test you didn't prepare for than to cheat to get a good grade, even if you don't get caught. Not bragging and rubbing it in someone's face that you won the game is more important than actually winning the game. And if you lose, there is such a thing as losing well by how you accept defeat and move forward. Integrity allows us to make the right calls in all these situations and more.

Jesus handled himself with integrity throughout the gospel, and his followers strive to live the same way. As Christians, making decisions where we show integrity is a smooth transition of showing people the impact Christ has in our life. On the other hand, if we constantly make decisions lacking integrity, we are cheapening our witness, and it will be very hard for others to see God from our lifestyle.

In your lifetime, you will experience many good and bad things, and you often will have no control over them. Sometimes the only thing you have control over is how you choose to react to what life throws your way. Will you handle your wins successfully? Will you let your defeats defeat you?

Integrity is a fancy word for having a Christlike heart. Remember this week to do your best to model Jesus Christ in your actions, decisions, and even in your innermost thoughts. It's hard, but you can do it!

REFLECTION QUESTIONS:

What does the word Integrity mean to you? What are the qualities of someone with integrity?

____
____
____
____
____
____
____
____

How did Jesus model a lifestyle of integrity for all of us? What is a characteristic of Jesus that you wish you had more of?

____
____
____
____
____
____
____
____

PRAYER:

Lord Jesus, please continue to shape me to be more and more like you every day. Holy Spirit transforms my heart to be more like that of God. Help me and direct me in every decision I make, every trial I face, and every problem I have to overcome. Help me handle everything with integrity. Amen.

WEEK 25: DOUBT IS OKAY

Reading Plan for NIV Scriptures:

DAY 1: MATTHEW 14:28-31 *(Jesus saved Peter when he doubted)*

DAY 2: MARK 9:21-24 *(Jesus can help us with our unbelief)*

DAY 3: MATTHEW 28:16-17 *(You can worship God and still doubt)*

DAY 4: JOHN 20:24-29 *(Thomas's faith grows because of his doubt)*

DAY 5: JUDE 1:22 *(Have mercy on people that doubt)*

DAY 6: 2 PETER 1:19 *(God's word pushes through the doubt)*

DAY 7: PSALM 50:15 *(Call on God when you have questions)*

WEEKLY COMMENTARY:

One of my favorite characters in the Bible is the disciple Thomas, but I never liked that we nicknamed him "Doubting Thomas."

Thomas doubted that Jesus had been raised from the dead, which I feel is a reasonable way to think. In my own life, I don't know a single person that was dead and now is not. To be fair, Thomas would have been around Jesus when he brought Lazarus back from the dead, so this wasn't the first time someone rose from death in Thomas's life.

When Jesus saw Thomas's doubt, he allowed him to feel the nail holes in his hands, and Thomas grew in his faith and worshiped Jesus. I have always wondered what his faith was like AFTER this moment in the Bible. I bet his faith was rock-hard and very difficult to budge. This probably was a huge moment in his own faith journey and one that he shared with a lot of people he witnessed. Thomas's story doesn't end with him doubting, so I don't like calling him Doubting Thomas. If anything, I choose to call him Certain Thomas because his doubt led to a stronger belief.

Know that you can have questions and doubts and still worship God and have faith too. Having faith does not mean that you have all the answers. Often times we need faith the most when we *don't* have the answers. Doubt is not meant to be the final destination of a concern you have.

When you doubt, use it to ask a question and find the answer. Pray that God guides your doubt to certainty. In my experience, when I do that, one of two things happens. Either God helps me find the answer to my question, which is always great. Or, God guides me to a greater truth about Him that helps me love God more, care about the doubt, and question less.

Oftentimes people have doubts or questions and are too afraid to address them, and the doubt festers into something worse. Or, sometimes, people voice their doubts or question, and another Christian doesn't respond in kind and loving way, which does more harm than good. Both of those are examples of how to NOT handle your questions.

It's okay to ask God questions; he's big enough for your doubts and uncertainty. It's okay to voice those concerns with other people. You can still love, worship, and have faith in God even if you don't have all the answers. In fact, God is so big that none of us will ever know everything about him. And that's okay!

REFLECTION QUESTIONS:

What is a question, concern, or doubt, you have about God, Christianity, the Bible, or Jesus?

____
____
____
____
____
____
____

When you have doubts, what are healthy ways to address them? Who can you go to with your questions, and who will safely address them?

____
____
____
____
____
____
____

PRAYER:

Thank you, Lord, for being bigger than my doubts and questions. Help me with my unbelief, and please use it to guide me to a deeper faith. Please guide me to the answers I am looking for or help me realize I don't need the answer I am asking for.
Amen.

WEEK 26: THE GIFT OF SINGLENESS

Reading Plan for NIV Scriptures:

DAY 1: 1 CORINTHIANS 7:7-8 *(Singleness is a gift from God)*

DAY 2: MATTHEW 19:12 *(Some people choose to be single)*

DAY 3: 1 CORINTHIANS 7:32-34 *(A single person can focus on God more)*

DAY 4: MATTHEW 7:7 *(Ask God for what you truly desire)*

DAY 5: PSALM 68:6 *(God provides a community for everyone)*

DAY 6: 1 CORINTHIANS 7:9 *(If you can't control your passions, get married)*

DAY 7: EXODUS 6:7 *(Single or not, we all have a relationship with God)*

WEEKLY COMMENTARY:

In 1 Corinthians, the apostle Paul calls singleness a *gift*, but I don't think I've ever met a middle schooler or high schooler that has ever considered being single a gift. Many adults don't, either. If Singleness is a gift, many of us would prefer to regift it to the boyfriend of our current crush!

I am sure you have met middle or high schoolers at your school or maybe even in your church who feel like they always have to have a girlfriend or boyfriend to be "Complete." You know people, and you might even be one of these people, that define their whole identity on who they are dating or whether or not they are dating someone.

But what if we thought more like Paul and considered singleness a gift?

There are a lot of positives to not being in a relationship. In 1 Corinthians, Paul informs us that single people are able to dedicate themselves more fully to the Lord. Dating and relationships, hopefully, lead to marriage, and in marriage, you no longer ask the question, "What's God's will for MY life" but instead have to ask, "What's God's will for OUR life." It can be argued that it is easier to be fully devoted to God when you aren't devoted to your significant other.

When you're single, it's easier to go when God calls you to go. Think about it if you're in a serious relationship right now: How hard would it be if God called you to be a missionary to the other side of the world and start tomorrow? As a single person, you have freedom that allows you an ease to the large commitments you are called to make.

This isn't an anti-marriage devotion. Marriage is great, and as a gift comes with its own blessings. Instead of hating on singleness or marriage, we should be encouraged to enjoy whatever season of life we are in now. You may grow up to be married, and I hope you enjoy the gift of marriage as much as God wants you to.

If you're single now or ever single, I also hope you enjoy that gift for as much blessing as God intends for you. This week, take time to appreciate that the only relationship we truly need to be complete is one with our Heavenly Father and Creator.

REFLECTION QUESTIONS:

When you think of being single, how does it make you feel? How important is it to you to be in a relationship?

____
____
____
____
____
____
____

In the Bible, Paul calls singleness a gift. Do you agree? What are some perks of being single as a Christian, or if you disagree, why?

____
____
____
____
____
____
____

PRAYER:

Thank you, God, for all the amazing gifts you bless me with every day. I pray that you help me be content in the season of life that I am in today. Help me feel complete in times when I am by myself because I know I am never truly by myself. You are always with me, and you're more than enough for me. When I struggle to remember this, please remind me. Amen.

WEEK 27: DATE INTENTIONALLY

Reading Plan for NIV Scriptures:

DAY 1: 2 CORINTHIANS 6:14 *(Don't date non-Christians)*

DAY 2: 1 CORINTHIANS 5:11 *(Have standards with who you date)*

DAY 3: 1 CORINTHIANS 13:4-7 *(Characteristics of Love)*

DAY 4: PROVERBS 18:22 *(Wives are blessings from God)*

DAY 5: PROVERBS 19:14 *(Prudent wives are from God)*

DAY 6: EPHESIANS 5:33 *(Love your wife/girlfriend as you love yourself)*

DAY 7: 1 CORINTHIANS 6:13 *(Don't be sexually immoral)*

WEEKLY COMMENTARY:

So many teenagers get into relationships because they want the social status it brings at school, or they want to feel loved or "complete," or they just want the physical benefits. There are plenty of terrible reasons to date someone and only a few really good ones. But the good reasons, though there are only a few, are incredibly valid.

Dating prepares us for marriage. If you are ever dating someone and realize this isn't a person you can marry, that is a fantastic reason to break up. The root point of marriage is to better see God through your love for this specific person. Your eventual wife should help you be a better Christian. Since dating is, in a sense, marriage practice, you should be striving to help your significant other know God better too.

One of the reasons teenagers get hurt so much when dating is that they have no standards for the kind of person they decide to date. It's okay to be picky when choosing a girlfriend. Your question shouldn't be, "Will she date me?" but "Should I date her?" You should have dealbreakers or characteristics that you won't budge on when looking for a partner.

Some of these standards you will figure out as you date people and relationships begin and end. Other standards you can keep from day one of dating. A great standard that will help you have a better experience when dating is to only date people with the same core, essential beliefs.

As a Christian, your faith and relationship with God should be incredibly important to you. It makes sense then that you shouldn't date someone who doesn't have or value a relationship with God. There is nothing wrong with being friends with a non-Christian, but it is okay to be more picky and specific with the kind of person that you would accept as a girlfriend or eventual wife.

Date intentionally. Don't just date because you don't like being alone or because everyone else is doing it. Suppose that's the reason you feel you have to be in a relationship. In that case, I am sorry that you may not be emotionally mature enough yet to be a good boyfriend. A potential girlfriend won't fulfil the needs you are experiencing.

Lastly, don't rush it. If you're in middle and high school and don't feel the desire to date, that is perfectly fine. You aren't weird, you aren't alone, and you might save yourself from a lot of pain. Date intentionally, or don't date at all.

REFLECTION QUESTIONS:

What are some of the reasons people start dating? Which reasons do you consider valid, and which ones do you think are wrong?

____
____
____
____
____
____
____
____

What are some standards you have set for yourself when it comes to dating and the kind of person you will date?

____
____
____
____
____
____
____
____

PRAYER:

God, as I consider dating, please give me wisdom and discernment to make good decisions. Help guide me to the person you want me to date, or help me know if I shouldn't date someone. I pray that you continue to develop me into the kind of person that makes a good boyfriend, and I pray for my future girlfriend and wife that you continue to develop her as well. Amen.

WEEK 28: HOW TO BE A GOOD BOYFRIEND

Reading Plan for NIV Scriptures:

DAY 1: 📖 EPHESIANS 5:21 *(Respect Christ by submitting to each other)*

DAY 2: 📖 EPHESIANS 5:25-28 *(Love your girlfriend like Christ loved the church)*

DAY 3: 📖 1 PETER 4:8 *(Above all, love each other)*

DAY 4: 📖 GENESIS 2:18 *(We need community)*

DAY 5: 📖 ECCLESIASTES 7:8-9 *(Do not be quick to anger)*

DAY 6: 📖 MATTHEW 7:12 *(Do to others as you would want done to you)*

DAY 7: 📖 1 PETER 3:7 *(Respect your girlfriend)*

WEEKLY COMMENTARY:

What makes someone a good boyfriend? If you asked this question in your school or church, you might get a variety of answers. There would be some good answers. "Being a good listener," "Being kind," "Being supportive," and "Being honest" are a few that come to mind. There might be some not-great answers. "Being buff," "Being cool," "Being popular," "Being someone that everyone else wishes they were dating."

The concept of boyfriends and girlfriends didn't exist during Bible days, so while there is no concrete advice given on how to date, we can make some strong assumptions based on the standards that are given for being a good husband.

After all, good boyfriends grow up to be good husbands.

A "husband or boyfriend trait" we see throughout the Bible is the importance of submitting to your wife (or girlfriend) as Christ submitted to the church. Christ put the church first, and in relationships, we must put the other first. (Girlfriends are also encouraged to do the same.) If you're not ready to be selfless and put your significant other's needs above your own, then perhaps you are not ready to be in a relationship.

Good boyfriends are honest and respectful. Good boyfriends respect their girlfriends' parents, even if she doesn't because that's an example of putting her needs above your own. Good boyfriends strive to be a Christian example in the kind of boyfriend they are because the most important aspect of any romantic relationship is that you are helping your mate know God better.

If you aren't helping your girlfriend know God better, then you aren't being as good of a boyfriend as you could be.

A lot of people get into relationships because they want to look more popular, because they don't like being alone, or just because they think the other person is really hot. When we date because of these reasons, we are cheapening the blessing of romantic relationships.

Have standards for who you date, and make sure you are dating for the right reasons. If you are in a relationship, take your role as a "Good Boyfriend" seriously because good boyfriends eventually grow up to be good husbands.

REFLECTION QUESTIONS:

Have you thought about your standards for the kind of girlfriend or wife you want in your life? List the qualities of your ideal mate here.

____

____

____

____

____

____

____

____

____

What standards do you have for yourself as a boyfriend/husband? How does Christ factor into you being this kind of person?

____

____

____

____

____

____

____

____

____

PRAYER:

Lord. all relationships are opportunities to share You with others, and that includes dating relationships as well. Please bless my dating relationships to help me be a light to my significant other. Jesus, please help me to put her needs above my own and strive to love her as much as You do. Amen.

WEEK 29: WHY WAIT?

Reading Plan for NIV Scriptures:

DAY 1: 1 CORINTHIANS 6:16-20 *(Honor God with your body)*

DAY 2: HEBREWS 13:4 *(Keep the marriage bed pure)*

DAY 3: 1 THESSALONIANS 4:3-6 *(Have self-control)*

DAY 4: GENESIS 2:24 *(Sex connects us spiritually)*

DAY 5: MARK 10:6-9 *(God intended sex for marriage)*

DAY 6: GENESIS 1:28 *(Sex is for making babies)*

DAY 7: COLOSSIANS 3:5 *(Put to death sexual immorality)*

WEEKLY COMMENTARY:

In my experience, the Church does a great job at telling teenagers that they need to wait to have sex until they are married, but they often neglect to share with you the strong arguments as to why this is a good idea. Let me share with you why God wants you to wait for marriage before you have sex

Sex is an intimate activity that connects us in a special way to our partner. Think about it this way: We have different forms of touch that establish different levels of intimate connection. A high five connects you to someone more than a head nod. Even more, than a high five would be a handshake. More than a handshake, a hug. (If you ever are away from home for a while and return, you don't greet your mom with a handshake, right?) More than hugs would be kisses…you probably hug many people in your family and probably don't kiss them. Even within a kiss, there are different levels to reflect different intimacy.

Sex is the most intimate act we can do with someone, and it shouldn't be an activity we share with just anyone. People drift apart for any number of reasons (if you have ever been in a break-up, you understand!), but if you have sex and then go your separate ways, *you're still connected on a spiritual level.* You may not know it now, but there may be many exes in your life that you will not want to stay connected with after your relationship ends.

Sex in the confines of a healthy marriage is a wonderful gift that connects you with your soulmate in the most beautiful way. God designed sex to make babies and to be a beautiful gift between spouses. When we misuse this gift in other settings, we do not appreciate it for its full God-intended value, and with sex, there are some very real consequences that I'd just assume you don't have to deal with.

And *that's* why God designed sex for marriage.

REFLECTION QUESTIONS:

What are your thoughts on sex? Do you agree with the Christian understanding that you should wait till marriage before having sex? Why or why not?

____
____
____
____
____
____
____

Have you thought about your future spouse? What are qualities that you hope they have? How important is it to your future marriage that you refrain from sex now?

____
____
____
____
____
____
____
____

PRAYER:

Thank you, Lord, for the gift of sex within the gift of marriage. I pray that you help me understand your wisdom as it pertains to sexual purity. I pray for my future wife. Please help me grow as a person daily so that I can be the best possible husband for her one day. Help me not give into temptation, and help me worship you through how I treat my body. Amen.

WEEK 30: HOW TO BE A WITNESS

Reading Plan for NIV Scriptures:

DAY 1: ROMANS 1:16 *(Do not be ashamed of the Gospel)*

DAY 2: 1 PETER 2:9 *(We are Chosen to share God with others)*

DAY 3: COLOSSIANS 1:28 *(We proclaim Jesus to others)*

DAY 4: ISAIAH 43:10 *(We are the Lord's witnesses)*

DAY 5: ROMANS 10:14 *(People hear about God from us)*

DAY 6: ROMANS 15:13 *(God will overflow through you)*

DAY 7: MATTHEW 10:20 *(Let the Holy Spirit speak through you)*

WEEKLY COMMENTARY:

Have you ever discovered a new favorite TV show, and then you felt the need to tell everyone you know about it? That is how I am with any new TV show, restaurant, or band I discover. It's something that is amazing in my life, and so now I feel the need to impart this great addition to someone else's life too.

The thing is, you can't MAKE them start watching the show, go to the restaurant, or listen to the band. All you can do is share your positive experience with the hopes that they take your word and try it out for themselves.

That is how you Witness. Your only job is to share your experience. Everything else is out of your control and not your responsibility.

God calls us to be Witnesses for Jesus Christ. As a witness, your job is to share what you have seen and experienced. In a courtroom, nobody expects the witness to settle the case. They are there solely to share what they know. It's up to the lawyers to convince the judge or jury, and ultimately the verdict comes down to their decision. The witness simply shares.

When you Witness to your friends and family about Jesus, all you need to do is tell them about the role of Jesus in your life and the amazing things that He has done for you. Share what you know, how you feel, and what you have seen. If they don't believe you, then you have done nothing wrong.

The Holy Spirit does the convicting. It's God's job to move through their heart through what you say. It's important for you to share your experiences with your faith so that the Holy Spirit has something to move through.

You may feel like it's a preacher's job to witness for Jesus, not yours. Here's the problem, though, some people can relate better to how you have experienced God than how your minister has. You have friends who may not care much about a preacher's witness. But maybe the way you experience God is something that they can relate to.

There is a good chance that you may be a better preacher and witness for Jesus for the people in your life than your actual minister is. Don't feel overwhelmed by that responsibility. Your only job is to witness and share how you have experienced God. The Holy Spirit will do the rest!

REFLECTION QUESTIONS:

How has God moved in your life? What are some of your favorite "God moments" or "God stories" that you have experienced?

____
____
____
____
____
____
____

Who in your life could you feel could be a Witness for Jesus? What are ways this week that you can witness this person?

____
____
____
____
____
____
____

PRAYER:

God, thank you for all the big and amazing ways you have moved in my life. Help me this week be a good witness of you to my friends, family, and everyone I come in contact with. Holy Spirit, give me the words to say and direct me to the right people that You want me to share Jesus with. Amen.

WEEK 31: FRIENDSHIP

Reading Plan for NIV Scriptures:

DAY 1: PROVERBS 27:9-10 *(A good friend is a blessing)*

DAY 2: 1 CORINTHIANS 15:33 *(A bad friend can corrupt you)*

DAY 3: COLOSSIANS 3:12-14 *(Qualities of a good friend)*

DAY 4: ECCLESIASTES 4:7-12 *(We are stronger with good friends)*

DAY 5: ROMANS 12:9-16 *(A good friend puts his friends first)*

DAY 6: PROVERBS 22:24-27 *(Have standards for yourself and your friends)*

DAY 7: PROVERBS 27:17 *(A good friend can make you better)*

WEEKLY COMMENTARY:

Would you rather have one really good friend or one hundred below-average friends?

As much as we fantasize about what it might be to be the most popular person in the world, with a large number of friends, the better option is to have at least one really good friend.

Good friends can be life-changing. A great friend can help make you a better person and can help you through the worst of times. Having good friends can make life more enjoyable because it's always more fun to share experiences with people you like and care about. Sometimes we may want to *be alone,* but none of us want to be *lonely.* Good friends are the perfect cure for loneliness.

Bad friends can be a different story altogether. The Bible tells us that bad company corrupts good character. As humans, it's not difficult to be influenced by people around us. If we're honest with ourselves, it's easier to give into sin than it is to live a holy life. (Notice I said *easier* and not *better.*) If our friends are always doing things they shouldn't, speaking poorly about others, or living in a way that doesn't honor God or represent their Best self, it's very tempting for us to do the exact same.

What kind of friend are you? Are you a positive influence on your friends? Do you help them be better and enjoy life more? Or are you someone that it's easy to *"slum it"* with? Are you encouraging or discouraging? Are you a good listener? Do people enjoy sharing life with you? Do you put your friends first, or are you selfishly only friends with people who help you do better?

As a Christian, it's as important to BE a good friend as it is to HAVE good friends.

This week, take some time and evaluate your relationships. How are you sharing Christ through your friendship? Are your friend's good influences and role models in your life? Who in your life could use a friend, and how can you be a good friend to them? Allow the Holy Spirit to move through these questions this week!

REFLECTION QUESTIONS:

What are important qualities that you look for in a friend? Who among your friends has these qualities?

____
____
____
____
____
____
____

How can you share Christ and make people's life better this week by being a good friend?

____
____
____
____
____
____
____
____

PRAYER

Dear Jesus, thank you for each and every one of my friends. I pray that you bless them and make your presence known in their lives. Please help me be a great friend to them and anyone else I know that needs a good friend. Holy Spirit, I ask you to move through my friendships in a way that allows me to share You more with everyone I know. God, if there is someone in my life that needs a friend, please direct me to them this week. Amen.

WEEK 32: YOU'RE BETTER THAN THAT

Reading Plan for NIV Scriptures:

DAY 1:  MATTHEW 5:28 *(Lust happens in the heart)*

DAY 2: 2 TIMOTHY 2:22 *(Flee from evil desires)*

DAY 3: 1 JOHN 2:16 *(Lust is not from God)*

DAY 4: PROVERBS 6:25 *(Don't lust in your heart)*

DAY 5: JAMES 1:13-15 *(God does not tempt you)*

DAY 6: 1 CORINTHIANS 6:9-10 *(Sin keeps us from the kingdom of God)*

DAY 7: GALATIANS 5:24 *(Christ saved you from your passions and desires)*

WEEKLY COMMENTARY:

Whenever I used to get in trouble, my parents would tell me, "You're better than this." I remember feeling so ashamed when I heard those words because I often knew they were right. Whatever mistake I was making, I often knew that I was above behaving in whatever way I was behaving.

If you choose to live a life devoted to Christ and following God's will, you are choosing to live a life that is better than worldly standards. The world has certain expectations that they settle for regarding teenage boys. You're supposed to be hormonal. You're supposed to be impulsive. You're supposed to be growing oafs that are dominated by your urges because "Boys will be boys," and you'll eventually grow out of it.

But Christ calls each and every one of you to be better than that.

The world says, "As long as you don't commit adultery or act inappropriately towards a woman, you aren't committing a sexual sin." Jesus tells us, "if you think about a woman lustfully, you have committed adultery in your heart."

The problem with lust is that it devalues the personhood of who we are looking at and is a way we let our most primal urges overtake our judgment and sound reasoning. Nobody has ever made better decisions when they've let their lust rule their lives.

Christ calls us to be better than our lustful and sinful nature. You should never be justifying lustfully looking at women as "Well, I'm only human" because you are cheapening what the power of the Holy Spirit can do through and in you. God calls you to be stronger than that and wants a better and more fruitful life for you.

Lusting is a sin, and Jesus died so that you are not ruled or bound by any of your sins. If it ever feels too hard to bear or like you can't overcome your lust, know that God does not allow us to handle more than we can bear. It may not seem like that sometimes, but the Bible is very clear: God is always with us and will help us through anything and everything we have to deal with. All you have to do is ask for His help, and you will receive it.

This week, if you are struggling with lust or any kind of sin that you feel is too powerful for you, remember that thanks to the blood of Jesus Christ, you are better than your sin. Sin no longer defines you and has no power over you. Don't let it rule your life; give your life to God instead.

REFLECTION QUESTIONS:

What are some of the biggest temptations in your life today? What are ways you can overcome these temptations, and how can God help you to do so?

____

____

____

____

____

____

____

____

How does choosing not to live lustfully or being overcome by any kind of sinful habit make you live a better and more Godly life? How is your life better by not sinning?

____

____

____

____

____

____

____

____

PRAYER:

God help me not be bound by sin. Jesus, thank you for dying for all my sins and giving me an opportunity to live a free and beautiful life not dictated by lust and other forms of evil that creep into my heart. Holy Spirit. Help guide me every day to resist my lustful desires, and help me strive to live a holier life every day. Amen.

WEEK 33: GOD IS SOVEREIGN

Reading Plan for NIV Scriptures:

DAY 1: COLOSSIANS 1:15-17 *(God created all things and held them together)*

DAY 2: PSALM 19:7-10 *(Everything about God is perfect)*

DAY 3: ROMANS 8:31-32 *(If God is with us, who can be against us?)*

DAY 4: LUKE 1:37 *(God's word never fails)*

DAY 5: PROVERBS 3:5-8 *(Trust in the Lord)*

DAY 6: HEBREWS 10:23 *(Hold on to the Hope God promises)*

DAY 7: ISAIAH 25:8-9 *(God is Sovereign)*

WEEKLY COMMENTARY:

When I was in 6th grade, I was on a recreation league soccer team that never lost a match for the entire season. For whatever reason, all of the best players in our league somehow winded up on the same team. (And somehow, I ended up on that team too!) It was a wonderful feeling going into every soccer game each week, *knowing* there was no chance that we would lose.

As Christians, we should find comfort and joy in the fact that we are on the winning team *with God*. God's perfect. God never fails. God is all-powerful. God has saved all of humanity from sin through his Son Jesus and continues to bless and move through the world today, doing miracles and changing lives. God is always moving and saving, no matter how bad things may get.

The Church has a fancy word to describe God's "undefeated" record, and the word is *sovereign*. To say that God is sovereign is to acknowledge that God is in control, will never fail, and is always there for us.

Imagine having to take a test for a really difficult class, but the professor who also wrote the textbook gets to take the test with you. It's a hard test, but you'll ace it with the professor's help! Imagine having to play a two-on-two basketball game with the two best players in your school, but your teammate is Michael Jordan. You'll win, for sure!

Sometimes life can be really tough. School can be stressful. Friends can let us down. People can be mean. Sometimes bad things happen outside of our control. Relatives get sick. Parents get divorced. Best friends move. Life can be challenging! Sadly, as you get older, it doesn't get any easier.

This week, take strength from this *fact*. Nothing you ever deal with can overpower God. God never loses; God can prevail through all circumstances. God has already won, and you're on God's team. Life and sin may bend you, but thanks to God, they can never break you. Find your strength in this truth: *Your God is Sovereign*.

REFLECTION QUESTIONS:

What is the hardest thing that you, or someone you know, has ever been through? Did you see God move in this circumstance? If so, how?

____
____
____
____
____
____
____
____

How does the truth that God is Sovereign mold how you look at hard circumstances, trouble, stress, and tragedy?

____
____
____
____
____
____
____
____

PRAYER

Majestic Father above, you are so powerful, and everything in existence is in your control. Thank you so much for always loving me and providing for me. I know that whatever I ever go through will never be too much for you. Please help me to remember to find my strength in you the next time I feel overwhelmed because I can do all things through, He who strengthens me. Amen!

WEEK 34: GRIEF IS OKAY

Reading Plan for NIV Scriptures:

DAY 1:  PSALM 46:1-3 (*God is our refuge and strength*)

DAY 2: MATTHEW 5:4 (*Mourners will be comforted*)

DAY 3: PSALM 48:14 (*God will guide us always*)

DAY 4: 2 CORINTHIANS 1:3-4 (*God is our comforter*)

DAY 5: JOHN 16:22 (*Grief is temporary*)

DAY 6: ROMANS 8:18 (*Our glory will outweigh our suffering*)

DAY 7: MATTHEW 11:28-30 (*Come to Jesus when you are burdened*)

WEEKLY COMMENTARY:

Has someone ever tried to give you a compliment, but it came out as an insult? Something like, "I don't like most of your shirts, but that one is nice!" Often when people lose a relative or are going through a traumatic experience, it's tempting to say comments with the hopes of being helpful that can, in fact, be very hurtful.

Funerals are the worst places to say, "Your loved one is in a better place." or, "I know things are bad now, but it will get better!" Those are true statements, but when people are grieving, they are not ready to hear them. It's important to note that whether you are the person speaking or you are the person grieving, we can't speak anyone *out of* grief.

Grief is okay. God is present in our grief. God comforts us in ways that nobody else can.

There is no pain like the loss of a loved one. Even if it's a grandparent that dies of old age, and you know it's their time, it still really hurts not to have them in our life. It's especially painful when tragic situations happen. The world is full of sin; sometimes, bad things happen, and there is nothing we can say or do to prevent it.

In times like this, no actions can be taken to fix the situation, and no words can be spoken that will make things better. The only fix for grief is often time. There is no time frame for grief, but things do get better eventually.

It's important to remember that in those times of grief, God is present during our brokenness. We may feel alone, but God is present throughout the whole situation. He will get us through our sadness, and He is present throughout it.

When words fail, God is there. Where there is nothing we can do, God is there, ready to comfort us. I hope you don't have many tragic times in your life, like the loss of a loved one, but know that when these times happen, you are NOT alone. God is 100% always with you and is ready to comfort you in times when everyone else's actions and words will fail.

If you are grieving, know that there is no right or wrong way to grieve. There is sadly also no time frame. Talk with who you need to talk to, do what you need to do, and know that God is with you.

REFLECTION QUESTIONS:

What are the worst ways to try to comfort someone when they are grieving? What are the best ways?

____
____
____
____
____
____
____

Have you had an experience with grief? If so, what was it like, and where did you see God in this experience?

____
____
____
____
____
____
____

PRAYER:

God, thank you for always being with us no matter what the circumstance. Please remind me of your presence in times of grief, and please help me point others to you when they are grieving. Thank you for always comforting us. Amen

WEEK 35: EVANGELISM

Reading Plan for NIV Scriptures:

DAY 1: 2 CORINTHIANS 5:20 *(We are Christ's ambassadors)*

DAY 2: 2 TIMOTHY 4:5 *(Keep your head in all situations)*

DAY 3: MATTHEW 9:37-38 *(The harvest is plentiful, and we are needed)*

DAY 4: MATTHEW 10:7 *(As you go, proclaim the message of God)*

DAY 5: LUKE 4:18 *(You are sent to proclaim freedom to others)*

DAY 6: 2 THESSALONIANS 2:14 *(Sharing Christ is sharing in God's glory)*

DAY 7: ISAIAH 12:4 *(Proclaim God's name to everyone you know)*

WEEKLY COMMENTARY:

When I was in my mid-twenties, I woke up and realized that I was surrounded by people that looked, acted, and spoke exactly as I did. While this may seem like it would be comforting, I found it very disconcerting. God has given us a very important mission to go and tell the world about Jesus Christ, how he came and died for our sins, and accepting that will save us so that we can have an amazing life and relationship with our loving heavenly father.

I realized that if I am around a bunch of people that already know this, then I am not really doing my job as a Christian, am I?

Evangelism is a fancy word for "spreading the gospel of Jesus Christ." Gospel is another fancy church word that literally means "Good News." So to evangelize is to share the good news of Jesus Christ with others.

What good news, you ask?

There is so much! Jesus died on the cross for our sins so that we could have a relationship with God. Jesus broke the chains that sin held on us, so we are now free to live our best lives and not be doomed to be dominated by our own sin. Jesus modeled a perfect and awesome life that we can live as well, which is so much better than any other kind of life we could try to live. After rising from the dead, Jesus ascended to Heaven and promised to one day return to us and bring us to Heaven with him. Also, before Jesus left, he gave us the greatest gift ever, which is the Holy Spirit.

As you can see from the above paragraph, we have a lot of good news to share with anyone and everyone. Are you sharing it with everyone you know?

Or does everyone you know already know it? If you were like me several years ago, and that's the case, let me encourage you to get out of your bubble and go meet new people that need to hear the good news of Jesus Christ.

Those people are out there, and their life would be so much better if they had Jesus. You can help with that! This week consider who God is putting on your heart to share His Good News with.

REFLECTION QUESTIONS:

Was there someone in your life that was instrumental in telling you about Jesus Christ and helping you become a Christian? Who was this person, and how did they do it?

____
____
____
____
____
____
____

Who is it in your life that you can share the Good News of Jesus Christ with? If you can't think of anyone, where could you go to meet someone?

____
____
____
____
____
____
____

PRAYER:

Dear Lord, help me find the people in my life that you want me to share your Good News With. Give me the words to say and the strength to be courageous enough to share. Help break me out of my comfort zone so that I can better share you with others. Amen.

WEEK 36: WHAT GOES IN MUST COME OUT

Reading Plan for NIV Scriptures:

DAY 1:  PROVERBS 4:23-27 *(Everything comes from your heart)*

DAY 2: LUKE 6:43-45 *(Good fruit comes from a good heart)*

DAY 3: MATTHEW 6:22-23 *(Our eyes are the lamp to our body)*

DAY 4: PSALM 101:2-4 *(Be careful to lead a blameless life)*

DAY 5: 1 CORINTHIANS 6:12 *(Everything is permissible but not beneficial)*

DAY 6: EPHESIANS 1:18 *(Live into the hope God called you to)*

DAY 7: ISAIAH 6:10 *(Lets your heart be healed)*

WEEKLY COMMENTARY:

What goes up must come down, and what goes in must come out. If you've ever gone to the bathroom, you understand this concept. If you've ever tried to eat healthily, you also understand this concept. You probably won't be very healthy if you eat nothing but junk food. If you have a very good diet, it will lead to a healthier lifestyle.

Our spiritual lives are no different. What we listen to, what we watch, the people we hang out with, and the messages we take in all influence who we are. This is why you are reading these weekly devotions. By reading scripture daily and reflecting on these words, you are taking time to put Godly thoughts into your heart. Having encouraging friends will help you be happier. Watching TV shows with inspirational messages will help you be in a better place emotionally.

The opposite can be true. Listening to music with crass language and negative messages will mess with how you speak and think. Hanging out with negative and insulting friends will hurt your self-esteem. Watching TV with profanity will make it easier for you to repeat it to others.

It's important to monitor the influences you have in your life. Who are your closest friends? What are you listening to? What are you watching? As a Christian, if these influences are not helping you, they are probably hurting.

It's also important to note that *you* are an influence on others. Are you a good, life-giving influence? Or are you someone that negatively influences others? Are your words encouraging, or do they bring others down?

This week, consider what you take in and how you impact others around you.

REFLECTION QUESTIONS:

What are the things in your life that influence you the most? Would you consider these positive or negative influences?

____
____
____
____
____
____
____
____

How are you a good influence on your family and friends? What specific ways can you help pour into their lives and improve them? (If this is a hard question to answer, change it to how COULD you positively influence the people in your life?)

____
____
____
____
____
____
____
____

PRAYER:

God, please give me the willpower to only take in the positive influences in my life. Please help me turn away from the negativity in the media and the negativity in people I know in my life. Please also help me be a positive influence on all my friends and my family. Amen!

WEEK 37: BREAKUPS

Reading Plan for NIV Scriptures:

DAY 1: 📖 JOHN 14:27 *(God never leaves us)*

DAY 2: 📖 PSALM 34:18 *(The Lord is close to the brokenhearted)*

DAY 3: 📖 PSALM 73:26 *(God is our strength when we have none)*

DAY 4: 📖 PSALM 147:3 *(God heals the brokenhearted)*

DAY 5: 📖 ISAIAH 43:1-4 *(You are precious and honored in God's sight)*

DAY 6: 📖 JONAH 2:2 *(Call to the Lord in your times of need)*

DAY 7: 📖 ROMANS 8:28 *(God works all things for good)*

WEEKLY COMMENTARY:

I remember the first time I was broken up with, in the 7th grade. It was at church camp, and she said, "God told me to break up with you because He wants me to be with Austin." We had only been together for two short days at church camp, but I was "in love," and I had never felt a heartache like this before.

Now, more than twenty years later, I am pretty confident that God had nothing to do with her decision. I think, more realistically, she thought Austin was better looking and discovered he was available.

That being said, God is present, even in our breakups.

Having your heart broken may be one of the emotionally painful experiences out there, and usually, it's one of the first big pains we deal with as people, which makes it feel even worse. In these painful times, don't turn away from God. Allow yourself to be comforted by God, to be in His presence.

A lot of people develop "being broken up with" habits like eating a lot of junk food or going out with friends to have a great time (to hopefully forget about their breakup). There are also a lot of habits people can get into when they are trying to handle the pain of a breakup. Instead of those, add these to your "post-breakup process." Instead of eating tons of junk food, spend tons of time in scripture and with God's word. In addition to spending time with your friends and family, make sure you are also spending time with God. Will this fix your breakup pain? No. Will it make it better? Yes!

God is still here during your breakups, and remember you are still a Christian and representing Him after a breakup too. So many people are tempted to villainize their exes and treat them unkindly. For some reason, being a jerk after a breakup is easier than just leaving each other alone. Remember, regardless of how you feel about someone you break up with or someone who dumps you, they are still a beloved child of God who has value and feelings. Treat them as such, and don't be a jerk!

Breakups are part of living in this world, and they aren't a fun part. Remember how you handle your breakup can be a way you share Jesus with other people, and also remember that God is always with you and ready to comfort you in your times of need.

REFLECTION QUESTIONS:

What are ways God can help you during times of breakup or heart-ache? What are ways you can connect with him?

____
____
____
____
____
____
____
____

What are ways you can be intentional about being a good Christian role model when you are broken up with and when you break up with someone?

____
____
____
____
____
____
____
____

PRAYER:

Thank you, God, for always loving me and being present in all times, the good, the bad, and the ugly. Thank you for providing me comfort and peace when my heart aches the most. Help me find my strength in you when I am struggling. Also, please help me to love others in all circumstances (even after break-ups) just like you love all of us always. Amen.

WEEK 38: WHO'S YOUR MASTER?

Reading Plan for NIV Scriptures:

DAY 1: 📖 2 PETER 2:1 (*There are false teachers and leaders out there*)

DAY 2: 📖 JOHN 1:49-51 (*Following Jesus leads to us seeing great things*)

DAY 3: 📖 MATTHEW 6:24 (*No one can serve two masters*)

DAY 4: 📖 1 CORINTHIANS 10:21 (*You can't serve the Lord and sin together*)

DAY 5: 📖 JOSHUA 24:15 (*Serve God intentionally*)

DAY 6: 📖 DEUTERONOMY 4:24 (*The Lord is a jealous God*)

DAY 7: 📖 ROMANS 6:16 (*Be obedient to God*)

WEEKLY COMMENTARY:

There is an old saying, "Stand for something or fall for anything." I think we can rephrase it to something that is as equally try "Stand with *someone* or fall for *anyone.*"

In the first Avengers movie, the villain Loki terrifies a crowd of people in New York City and forces them to bow to him. As everyone is kneeling, Loki yells at the crowd, "Does this not feel natural!?!"

Loki is no role model, and he's definitely not God, but he wasn't necessarily 100% wrong in this quote. It is 100% natural for every human to have a master. As a human race, we are made to want to be ruled or led by someone or something.

Think about it. It's natural to look up to people you respect and want to be exactly like them. The role of an important coach, teacher, or leader of some form is so important because a leader can do so much good (or damage). We live our lives governed by something or someone.

It could be the love of money. Or it could be the love of success or popularity. Your master could be your future (Everything you do now is dictated by the goal you have set for yourself in the future). It could even be your diet. (Everything you eat and do is dictated by staying in shape you deem appropriate and healthy.)

Or, your master could be God.

Some of the masters we choose for ourselves aren't inherently terrible, but they are nowhere near as good of a master as God is. When we follow God and make Him the ultimate authority of our life, that is the first step to being the best version of ourselves. God will never leave you or forsake you and knows everything that is best for you. Any other master, even with the best intentions, can steer you wrong. God never will fail you.

Unfortunately, the Bible is very clear. You cannot have two masters. You cannot serve both God and money. You can't live a holy life and a sinful life. You either give Jesus all your heart, or you haven't given Him your heart yet.

This week consider who your master is and is your master the best possible ruler for your life and heart. I'll go ahead and give you a hint. If your master *isn't* God, then you could do way better for yourself.

REFLECTION QUESTIONS:

What do you think about the statement, "Everybody has a master." Do you agree or disagree? Who or what is your master, and how does that impact your life?

____
____
____
____
____
____
____
____

If you consider God to be your Master, is there anything that you are still holding onto that you haven't fully given to him yet? What are the steps you can take this week to fully submit to God?

____
____
____
____
____
____
____
____

PRAYER:

God, I give you my whole heart and everything I am. Help me each day to learn to fully submit to you in every aspect of my life. Search my heart, oh Lord, and help me see if there is anything I am still keeping from You. If there is something, please give me the strength to give it up to you. Thank you, Lord Jesus, for all that you do for me. Amen.

WEEK 39: WISE GUYS

Reading Plan for NIV Scriptures:

DAY 1: EPHESIANS 5:15-17 *(Make the most of every opportunity)*

DAY 2: MATTHEW 7-24-29 *(Build your life on Jesus's teachings)*

DAY 3: JAMES 3:13-18 *(Worldly wisdom is inferior to God's wisdom)*

DAY 4: COLOSSIANS 2:8 *(Don't be led astray by worldly thinking)*

DAY 5: JAMES 1:5 *(Ask God for wisdom, and He will provide)*

DAY 6: 1 CORINTHIANS 1:20-22 *(Worldly wisdom is foolishness to God)*

DAY 7: PROVERBS 2:6 *(Wisdom leads to knowledge and understanding)*

WEEKLY COMMENTARY:

Wisdom and knowledge are not the same things. Knowledge requires knowing facts and information. Wisdom is more abstract. It's how you choose to use your knowledge based on your values, and it takes into account your beliefs, influences, and in general, your core beliefs.

You want to be wise, but where are you getting your wisdom? There is worldly wisdom, and there is Godly wisdom. Worldly wisdom comes in many shapes and forms and changes frequently based on the times that we live in. Godly wisdom remains true no matter what time we live in and frequently clashes with the ideals of worldly wisdom.

The world may tell you it's wise to live only for yourself, striving to work one hundred hours a week to get the best-paying job so you can buy all kinds of houses and cars to make yourself happy. Godly wisdom teaches that worldly things all fade and money can't buy happiness.

Worldly wisdom may tell you that you should do what makes you happy, regardless of who it impacts and what it costs (other people). Godly wisdom teaches that the secret to a happy and meaningful life is serving others as Jesus did. We are most fulfilled when we serve God by serving others.

These are just two examples of the constant mixed messages you will receive in this world regarding what truly equates to legitimate wisdom. There is always someone out there, whether it's your parents, teachers, coaches, ministers, maybe even strangers at the grocery store, or whoever, that is going to advise you on the wisest way to live.

Some of these voices you should definitely listen to. (Probably not the stranger at the grocery store). But the most important voice you should listen to is God's voice. It's important to know scripture and understand God's ways and what He expects from us so that as you grow to be wiser, you are following the correct kind of wisdom and not the cheap one that the world offers.

"Looks like we have a wise guy over here, eh?" Yes, but *what kind of* wise guy?

REFLECTION QUESTIONS:

Who in your life would you consider to be the wisest person? What about them earns them this title, in your opinion? Why do you consider them to be wise?

____

____

____

____

____

____

____

What are "Worldly wisdom" examples you have heard of, and what are "Godly wisdom"? Does Godly wisdom seem better to you? Why or why not?

____

____

____

____

____

____

____

PRAYER:

Lord, please bless me with wisdom to know you better. Please direct my paths and help me discern how to best live my life as you intend for me. I know your ways are best, so please give me the guidance needed to be the wisest self possible. Thank you for the gift of the Bible and the wise words you have shared through it. Amen.

WEEK 40: POSITIVE PEER PRESSURE

Reading Plan for NIV Scriptures:

DAY 1:  1 PETER 3:13-17 *(If you suffer for doing right, you are blessed)*

DAY 2: PROVERBS 13:20 *(Walk with the wise and become wise)*

DAY 3: GALATIANS 1:10 *(Try to please God, not people)*

DAY 4: 1 CORINTHIANS 10:13 *(You won't be tempted with more than you can handle)*

DAY 5: PROVERBS 1:10 *(Don't give into sin)*

DAY 6: ACTS 5:29 *(Obey God, not people)*

DAY 7: JAMES 1:12-15 *(God is never the one tempting you)*

WEEKLY COMMENTARY:

You should care about what other people think about you.

Does that sentence sound off or weird to you? I imagine as a teenager, you have heard many messages about how you shouldn't give in to peer pressure and you should try not to worry about what others think about you. There is lots of truth to both those statements, but here's a bit of a different message for you to think about.

In Paul's letters, he spends a lot of time encouraging Christians to live well and be positive role models for Christ in all parts of life. He encourages them to live in such a way that others want to worship the same God as them, and thus, he encourages the Church to *care* about what others think.

Don't let that contradict other positive messages you have heard in the past. You shouldn't look for validation in your friends or the "popular kids" in school. You shouldn't change aspects of your looks or personality to fit in with a certain group. You definitely should not give in to peer pressure and do or say something that you know is wrong just so somebody will accept you.

The only validation you need that you matter is from God, and that's something you already have and can never lose.

That being said, as a Christian, you should feel pressured to live a life where others see Jesus through you. The word Christian literally means "Little Christ," and all of us should strive to be "Little Christs" to the world in everything we do.

You should feel pressured to not cuss and be nice to everyone so that they admire your faith and lifestyle. You should go out of your way to love people whom the rest of the world deems unloveable because they need Jesus too. You should forgive radically because Jesus commands you to. As a Christian, you should feel pressured by the Bible and other Christians to live a holy life set apart from God. You should feel that pressure, and hopefully, it helps you grow into the best version of yourself.

Should this "good peer pressure" make you hate yourself for not being perfect? Absolutely not! God gives you grace, and you should give it to yourself too. Should this "good peer pressure" push you to be a little better every day? Yes. With help from the Holy Spirit, you can grow a little every day!

I hope this week you see ways that you have grown recently and ways that you can continue to grow.

REFLECTION QUESTIONS:

What are ways that you feel pressured by your peers? Do you ever feel influenced to say or do something you know you shouldn't? When does this happen, and how do you resist it?

____
____
____
____
____
____
____
____

Is there anyone in your life who pressures you to be a better person? Do you have any "Positive Peer Pressure" in your life?

____
____
____
____
____
____
____
____

PRAYER:

Thank you, Jesus, for leading a life that shows us the correct way to handle every situation we ever will be in. Please help me live my life in a way that represents you well. Please help me resist the pressure to live in an ungodly way, and please continue to pressure me through your Word and through positive influences in my life to live a Godly life. Holy Spirit, mold me this week to be a better version of myself. Amen.

WEEK 41: HOW TO LOVE THE JERKS

Reading Plan for NIV Scriptures:

DAY 1: 1 CORINTHIANS 13:1-3 *(Love is more important than talent and knowledge)*

DAY 2: PROVERBS 18:13 *(Listen before you answer)*

DAY 3: MATTHEW 5:47 *(Build relationships with those different than yourself)*

DAY 4: PROVERBS 15:1 *(Respond gently instead of with harsh words)*

DAY 6: EPHESIANS 4:31-32 *(Get rid of every form of malice)*

DAY 6: MATTHEW 18:15-17 *(How to deal with a friend living in sin)*

DAY 7: ROMANS 14:1 *(Accept others instead of quarreling with them)*

WEEKLY COMMENTARY:

When I was in school, there was nothing I hated more than group projects. The teacher would always assign me to specific groups, and I never felt like I did the appropriate amount of work. Either I did the whole project, or I sat back and let someone do all the work for me. It was always the worst being put into a group for a project with people I didn't like. Ordinarily, I could just not associate with these people, but since we had a group project to do, I now *had* to talk to them.

As Christians, sometimes we have to accept that, in a way, Jesus calls us all into a group project together. There are 7 billion people on this planet, and you don't have to like or agree with every single one of them, but if you're a Christian, Jesus commands you to *love* them. One of the hardest parts of being a Christian is loving someone you think is wrong or someone who you think is a jerk.

Like many difficult things, loving others is worth it in the end. It is nearly impossible to share Jesus with someone who feels unloved. There is so much truth to the old saying, "People don't care about what you know until they know how much you care." If you ever want to change someone's mind, help them move past their faults, or share Jesus with them, you must start from a place of love.

Remember that Jesus's greatest commandment wasn't to fix everyone's bad behavior or correct everyone's wrong beliefs. Jesus doesn't expect us to perfect all the wrongs in the world, starting with the jerks we see at school or walking around in our lives. Jesus's greatest commandment was just one word, "Love."

Loving the "jerks" in the world can look different depending on the circumstances. Sometimes loving jerks look like going out of your way and comfort zone to establish a friendship with them. Sometimes it's speaking up in a fashion that treats them like a human but hopefully also corrects them as well. Sometimes it knows the right times to keep your comments to yourself.

We all have those "Jerks" in our world. They may go to our school, be in our family, or attend our church. You may see them frequently or hardly at all. No matter who they are or how much you see them, Jesus calls you to Love them. This week, go out of your way to love someone you deem "unloveable."

REFLECTION QUESTIONS:

What ways can you show Christlike love with people you don't like, disagree with, or have trouble being around?

____
____
____
____
____
____
____
____

Who are specific people in your life that you have problems with? What are those problems, and how can you share the love of Jesus with them this week?

____
____
____
____
____
____
____
____

PRAYER:

Lord, help me every day to learn to love others more as you do. Help me be able to see each person I interact with as you see them. Remind me of their value in your eyes, and help me see and appreciate their worth as well. Give me patience in the times that I really need it. Amen!

WEEK 42: STANDING FIRM FOR GOD

Reading Plan for NIV Scriptures:

DAY 1:  REVELATION 2:2-3 *(Persevere through hardships for God's name)*

DAY 2: JAMES 5:11 *(Persevering for God leads to blessings)*

DAY 3: JAMES 4:15-17 *(It is a sin to know good and not do it)*

DAY 4: 1 THESSALONIANS 5:21 *(Hold on to what's good)*

DAY 5: 2 CORINTHIANS 10:5 *(Break down any thought that is not of God)*

DAY 6: JOHN 7:17 *(Always choose God's will)*

DAY 7: MATTHEW 5:19 *(Anyone who follows God's commands is great)*

WEEKLY COMMENTARY:

Jesus was loving, kind, forgiving, and gentle, but he was not passive or a doormat. Jesus said what needed to be said when it needed to be spoken. He never steered away from conversations where He spoke out about God or against sin. When Jesus Christ saw wrong in the world, he spoke against it. He loved everything He did, but Jesus stood firm for God.

And as Paul said in Philippians, our life and attitude should be the same as Christ Jesus.

How do you handle the situation when you see someone being unkind to another person? Do you stand up for the person? Do you stay silent? Hopefully, you don't join in to be accepted by or "safe from" the bully.

How do you respond when someone shares something untrue about God or Christianity? Do you speak up? Do you share your opinions and thoughts? Or do you stay quiet and assume someone else will say something if it needs to be said?

The Bible teaches us that we are called to speak up for God and be assertive with how we share Jesus with others. It should always be done out of love, so hopefully, you aren't beating anyone upside the head with a Bible or calling them weirdos for not being a Christian. It's great if you aren't misrepresenting Christ, but how are you representing Him?

The Bible also teaches us that we will be blessed beyond measure when we are bold and firm in our faith. In my experience, there is nothing like having a good conversation with someone about God or taking the opportunity to stand up for the right cause in Jesus's name.

Let's be honest; in today's day and age, so many people are representing Christianity in Jesus's name that we *need you* to be comfortable sharing God in loving and assertive ways with others.

Take time this week to look at all aspects of your daily life. Are you standing firm for God when someone needs to stand firm? If not, how can you start being assertive with your faith?

REFLECTION QUESTIONS:

What are all the ways people "stand firm" for God or their faith that you think is wrong or that misrepresent Christ and Christianity?

____
____
____
____
____
____
____

What are the CORRECT ways to stand firm for God, and when are the times that you need to stand up for your faith the most?

____
____
____
____
____
____
____

PRAYER:

Lord Jesus, give me the strength to stand up for you when nobody else will. Give me a loving heart and correct words to say, as I am assertive in my faith. Direct others to me that I can help encourage in their faith, and Holy Spirit encourage me to keep going even when it's hard. Amen.

WEEK 43: THE BLESSING OF YOUR WORDS

Reading Plan for NIV Scriptures:

DAY 1: 1 THESSALONIANS 5:11 *(Encourage and build others up)*

DAY 2: COLOSSIANS 4:6 *(Let your conversations be full of grace)*

DAY 3: PROVERBS 10:20-21 *(Your words can nourish many)*

DAY 4: COLOSSIANS 3:15-17 *(Use words to teach others)*

DAY 5: PSALM 19:14 *(Let your words be pleasing to God)*

DAY 6: 1 CHRONICLES 16:34-36 *(Use words to pray and thank God)*

DAY 7: ROMANS 10:9-10 *(Use words to declare that Jesus is your Savior)*

WEEKLY COMMENTARY:

Often we are taught to be careful with our words and not use them to hurt others. Don't gossip, don't insult someone, and don't lie. These are all good teachings, and often a lesson on words is focused on how NOT to speak.

But this week, consider *what a gift* your words can be. Words can encourage, they can teach, can thank, can compliment, and they can heal. God can shine through and bless others through what you choose to say.

If you have ever had an amazing teacher, read an encouraging letter, or were given a fantastic piece of advice, then you know how powerfully *good* words can be. As a Christian, don't settle for just choosing not to lie, insult, or gossip. Instead, make it a point to use your words to point others to God.

Speaking of God, have you ever thought about the important part words play in our relationship with Him? We pray to God with our words, and we thank Him verbally. Additionally, an important part of becoming a Christian is *professing* faith in Jesus Christ. When we *call* on Jesus, He will come and save us.

Words are amazing and powerful blessings, and our words can make such a positive difference in the lives of others. This week be intentional, not just about what you *don't* say, but what you *do* say. Your words can change someone's week for the better and maybe their life.

REFLECTION QUESTIONS:

What is the nicest or most impactful thing someone has ever spoken to you about? What did they say, and how did God use it to change your life?

____
____
____
____
____
____
____
____

Who are three people in your life this week that you can use your words to bless? In the space provided, write down their names and what you should say to them.

____
____
____
____
____
____
____
____

PRAYER:

Thank you, God, for the blessing of communicating with you through words. I pray that you use what I say this week to be a light and encouragement to everyone I come into contact with. I pray that if someone needs a compliment, a good piece of advice, or wants to talk about You in any kind of way, you send me to them. Please give me the right words to speak, and let what I say be a blessing to those around me. Amen!

WEEK 44: NO OFFENSE

Reading Plan for NIV Scriptures:

DAY 1:  PROVERBS 4:24 *(Don't participate in a perverse or corrupt talk)*

DAY 2: EPHESIANS 5:3-4 *(Don't participate in the foolish talk or coarse joking)*

DAY 3: 1 PETER 3:10 *(Don't lie)*

DAY 4: JAMES 1:26 *(Be mindful of what you say)*

DAY 5: JAMES 3:3-12 *(Even small words can have a significant impact)*

DAY 6: EPHESIANS 4:29 *(Use your words for healing, not hurting)*

DAY 7: MATTHEW 15:10-11 *(Your words can defile you)*

WEEKLY COMMENTARY:

Any time you join a group, team, or organization, there usually are standards or a code of conduct that you are strongly encouraged, maybe even forced, to live by. I had worked at churches before that made me sign contracts saying I would never drink in public. Most high school sports will tell you that you will be kicked off the team if your grades drop at a certain point.

While Jesus doesn't make us follow a certain set of rules or standards before He saves us from sin, there is a strong expectation that, as Christians, we will live in a way that reflects Christ well to others. The Bible is very clear in numerous scriptures that we need to watch what we say and avoid offensive language.

If you are like I was when I was a teenager, it might seem a bit overwhelming to follow everything the Bible has to say about what we shouldn't say. No cussing; that was pretty easy for me. No coarse jokes...okay, *but what about the really funny ones*? No foolish talk...uh oh, I might be in trouble now!

The key for us is to remember that God wants us to use our words to build others up, worship Him, and share Jesus with others. If your words are doing the opposite, then that's where there is a serious problem.

A great rule of thumb is to ask yourself, "Is what I am saying offensive to someone?" If it is, then there is a very strong chance that you should probably not say it. Even if certain words or phrases don't bother you personally, if you know it hurts someone else, don't use those words around that person. By doing this, you love them with what you say (and what you don't), and loving others is one of the best ways that we can worship God.

This week take a closer look at everything you say. Do you complain a lot? Do you share a lot of offensive jokes? Do you insult people or whine? There are many ways we can use our words to not glorify God. As you grow, strive to get rid of those ways of speaking and replace them with using your words to honor, glorify, and share God.

REFLECTION QUESTIONS:

Think about the people in your life. Do you know anyone that bothers you by the way they speak or what they say? What is it about them or their words that bother you, and why?

____

____

____

____

____

____

____

Consider how you speak. Are there any ways that your words could be considered offensive to others or God? How can you get rid of this talk or change it to something better?

____

____

____

____

____

____

____

PRAYER:

Lord, please help protect my mouth this week from the offensive language of any form. If I am tempted to gossip, stop me. If I am tempted to say something mean, replace those words with a compliment. If I am tempted to lie, motivate me to live in truth. Help my words point people to you instead of pushing them away. Amen!

WEEK 45: DEALING WITH CONFLICT

Reading Plan for NIV Scriptures:

DAY 1: 📖 JOB 2:11-13 *(Be present with hurting friends)*

DAY 2: 📖 JAMES 5:13-16 *(Pray for your friends in trouble)*

DAY 3: 📖 MATTHEW 5:9 *(Peacemakers are blessed)*

DAY 4: 📖 LUKE 17:3 *(If a friend wrongs you, rebuke and forgive them)*

DAY 5: 📖 HEBREWS 12:14-15 *(Make every effort to live at peace with everyone)*

DAY 6: 📖 MATTHEW 5:23-24 *(Resolve conflict with friends before worship)*

DAY 7: 📖 1 CORINTHIANS 12:25-27 *(Strive for unity with everyone)*

WEEKLY COMMENTARY:

In middle school, I had a best friend named Brandon. Brandon and I had been friends since kindergarten and did as much as we could together. Even when we ended up going to different schools, we would find ways to hang out every weekend as much as possible.

Brandon and I didn't fight much, but when we did, it was brutal. We'd go weeks without talking, and then one of us would eventually make the first move to resolve or move past the issue. My mom had always said, "the greater the friendship, the greater the fights." She told me if a friendship is really worth it, you'll work through the conflict and be better friends because of it. If the friendship isn't worth it to you, it'll die when the issue comes.

Christians are called to be peacemakers and do what we can to live in peace with everyone. That being said, issues will occur in any relationship. Sometimes people are jerks, and sometimes *we're* a jerk. Whenever a fight arises between you and someone else, you have an opportunity to work through the problem to something greater.

There are many good and bad ways we can handle conflict. We can ignore it. We can get angry and yell at the person we're in a fight with. We can end friendships. We can never talk to people again. We can never address the problem, push it deep down inside, and risk being bitter about it for a long time. As you might have gathered, these are all terrible ways of handling conflict.

Or, we can do our best to work our issues out when they arise in relationships. We can talk. We can listen. We can go the extra mile. We can give each other space but then return. We can try again. We can forgive. We can move forward and learn from our mistakes. We can work through conflict and create space to become better people when it comes.

If you and a friend get in a fight this week, don't write them off. Perhaps God wants to use this issue to make you two better people with a deeper friendship.

REFLECTION QUESTIONS:

What is the biggest conflict you have ever had with a friend? Did God work through that situation?

____
____
____
____
____
____
____

What are healthy ways that you can work to resolve conflict when fights among friends and family happen?

____
____
____
____
____
____
____
____

PRAYER:

God help me be a peacemaker in my community. Help me be the person who resolves issues instead of starting them. Give me the right words to say to calm my friends when needed or rebuke them when I have to. Holy Spirit, move through my friendships so that I can share Jesus with everyone I come in contact with. Amen.

WEEK 46: THE LEAST OF THESE

Reading Plan for NIV Scriptures:

DAY 1: MATTHEW 25:34-45 *(Jesus calls us to care for everyone Din need)*

DAY 2: DEUTERONOMY 10:18-19 *(God cares for all "outsiders")*

DAY 3: COLOSSIANS 4:5 *(Make the most of every opportunity with outsiders)*

DAY 4: DEUTERONOMY 15:7-11 *(Give generously to the poor and needy)*

DAY 5: PSALM 41:1-3 *(God blesses those who care for the needy)*

DAY 6: PROVERBS 3:27-28 *(Don't withhold from helping others in need)*

DAY 7: ROMANS 12:16 *(Live in harmony with those in "low position")*

WEEKLY COMMENTARY:

40 "The King will reply, 'Truly I tell you, whatever you did for one of the least of these brothers and sisters of mine, you did for me.'

-Matthew 25:40

When Jesus talks about caring for the "Least of these," who is he talking about? If you see someone who doesn't have food or shelter, that person is the "least of these." If you meet someone who doesn't have any friends or is uncomfortable in a social situation, that person is the "least of these." If you meet a bully who is mean to others because of damage that someone else caused him or her, they are also the "least of these." Anyone who is lacking at any given point can be considered a "least of these." And whatever we do for the least of these, we are also doing for Jesus.

When I was in middle school, I moved to a new state and a new school. I went from knowing everybody in my middle school to knowing nobody. I remember at my old school, I never noticed the new kids or the people sitting by themselves because I was always busy hanging out with my friends. After I moved, I became the new kid with no friends and felt what it was like to be invisible in the lunchroom, and I didn't like it. I went from not noticing the people in need to becoming the person in need.

That experience taught me that we all, at one point, are in need and looking for someone to care for us, which makes none of us better than anybody else. The one thing we all have in common constantly is that each and every person that exists has existed, or ever will exist, is deeply loved by Jesus. No matter what you need in life, you'll never need God's love because you already have it and will never lose it!

Our response to Jesus's great love is to love Him back. One of the best ways to show love to someone is to care about what or who they care for. In this case, there is nothing Jesus loves more than all of us. So when you care for the people Jesus cares for, you are also showing love and care for Jesus.

Who is it in your life that really needs to be seen and provided for? Who is the "least of these" that God has put in your orbit? What is something this week you can do to take care of them? Whatever you do for the least of these, you are doing for Jesus!

REFLECTION QUESTIONS:

Has there ever been a time when you have been a "Least of These"? What was that experience like, and who was there to help provide for you?

____
____
____
____
____
____
____
____

Who is it around you that is in need, and are there ways that you can help provide for them?

____
____
____
____
____
____
____
____

PRAYER:

Thank you, Jesus, for loving me and caring for me no matter what I do or what happens in my life. Thank you for dying on the cross for my sins and saving me. I want to pray for all the people in need and thank you for providing for them as you provide for me. Please direct me, Lord, this week to someone in need and give me the strength, wisdom, and knowledge of how I can help be there for them. Amen!

WEEK 47: GOD IS ALWAYS WITH US

Reading Plan for NIV Scriptures:

DAY 1: GENESIS 28:15 *(God is with us wherever we go)*

DAY 2: ISAIAH 43:18-19 *(Don't dwell on the past)*

DAY 3: PROVERBS 23:18 *(We have hope in the future)*

DAY 4: PSALM 32:8 *(God will teach and guide us)*

DAY 5: EXODUS 23:20 *(God is present everywhere before come)*

DAY 6: DEUTERONOMY 31:8 *(God will never leave or forsake you)*

DAY 7: ISAIAH 32:18 *(God's people live in peace)*

WEEKLY COMMENTARY:

I have had to move to a lot of different places in my life. It's hard because I'll make friends, get close to them, and then feel like I have to leave them to go somewhere else. Also, I get used to whatever town I am living in. I know where the grocery stores are, my favorite coffee shop, and of course, where the best burger place is in town. And then, when you move, you have to rediscover everything all over again!

One of the first hardest circumstances many of us have to deal with is when we have the first big move. For some, you have to move during middle or high school, and it's a really hard experience. For many, there is a big move that happens after high school. As adults, you may have to move jobs or to new states to follow your career. Moving is a part of life. Even if you stay in the same place for your entire life, things change, friends may move, and circumstances "move" around you, which creates the same unsettling experience.

God is always with us, even when we find ourselves in new and unsettling parts of life. When you're at a new school, God is with you. God is present when you find yourself in a room with nobody you know. When all your friends move, but you have to stay, God is also still there with you. God will never leave or forsake you, and sometimes we have to hold on to that promise in tough new circumstances.

This is silly, but whenever I got homesick after moving, I had a cheap fix that helped me feel better, at least for a little bit. I would go visit the nearest Walmart to do my grocery shopping. No matter what city or state you live in, Walmart is always the same. In a new town where I didn't know where anything was, I could at least go to Walmart and know where all the items were located. In times of change, Walmart became my constant.

Don't settle for letting Walmart be your constant. Instead, God is a way better constant! When you move to a new place, God has already been there. When you are in a new situation that makes you a little nervous, God is there, ready to comfort and guide you. You will never go to a place that God hasn't already been and is currently.

God is forever and never changes, even when everything else in your life has.

REFLECTION QUESTIONS:

Have you ever had to experience a moving experience, a new school, or some big life change that made you nervous? What was that experience like, and how did God move through it?

____

____

____

____

____

____

____

____

How can you depend on God and find strength in Him when you find yourself in new and maybe scary circumstances?

____

____

____

____

____

____

____

____

PRAYER:

Thank you, Lord, for being my constant and my strength. Thank you for guiding me and staying with me no matter where I go or what I do. Help me this week to find peace in your presence, no matter where I am. Help me not be scared of the new and unknown and instead find beauty and purpose in it. Amen.

WEEK 48: LIFE ON HARD MODE

Reading Plan for NIV Scriptures:

DAY 1: 2 TIMOTHY 3:12 *(Living a Godly life leads to persecution)*

DAY 2: LUKE 9:1-6 *(If you aren't welcomed, move on)*

DAY 3: LUKE 9:23-26 *(Take up your cross daily)*

DAY 4: PSALM 41:7-13 *(God will protect you)*

DAY 5: 2 CORINTHIANS 4:8-9 *(We are pressed, but not crushed)*

DAY 6: PHILIPPIANS 4:12-13 *(You can do all things through God)*

DAY 7: 1 PETER 5:10 *(God will restore you)*

WEEKLY COMMENTARY:

Whenever I find a video game I really like, I beat it first on an easy setting, and I'll try it on the harder settings. I love playing games in the hard mode because while they are more challenging, you usually get better rewards, more points, or "better stuff" in the game. It's very satisfying to me, even if the game is more challenging that way.

If anyone ever has told you are living a Christian life is easier than not being a Christian, they either lied to you or were mistaken. Life for Christ is better and more satisfying for sure, but one word that would not describe the Christian life is…Easy.

Jesus is very clear in the Bible. If you follow him, you will be persecuted. Christianity is a radical way of life that teaches the importance of loving everyone, treating everyone justly and fairly, and putting others before yourself. Christianity also claims that God is the master of everything, and we must live by his plan, not our own. In a world that teaches that right and wrong are relative, God's law teaches that His ways are absolute and the best. Following Christ's teaching will absolutely put you on a path towards opposition from others, sometimes even with your friends.

And that's okay.

The Bible also teaches us that God will provide for us. God is enough for you. God will shine through you. No matter what problems come your way, God will prevail, and you're on God's team, so you will prevail too. Sometimes Christians need to oppose what's going on for the sake of other people, and God will always deliver you.

Sometimes there is a wrong message floating around, and it's the job of a Christian to preach the right message. Don't worry; they aren't your words but God's words. And God's words can't be unheard or ignored.

The Christian life is definitely hard, and there will be opposition. The rewards far outway the challenge, though. The rewards are changing people's lives for the better, pleasing your Lord and God, and living a life full of joy and purpose, unlike any other option.

Don't be afraid; go ahead and live your life in Hard Mode. It'll be worth it!

REFLECTION QUESTIONS:

What are some of the hardest parts of following God or being a Christian? What makes them so challenging?

____
____
____
____
____
____
____
____

Why do you think living a Christian life is worth it, regardless of the difficulty?

____
____
____
____
____
____
____
____

PRAYER:

Bring it on, Lord! I know that following you will be challenging, and conflict may arise with the world because Your ways are different and better than that of man. If that's the case, I proudly pray, "Bring it on!" Thank you, Lord, for providing me, protecting me, and delivering me from whatever challenges come my way. Amen.

WEEK 49: ENJOYING SALVATION TODAY

Reading Plan for NIV Scriptures:

DAY 1: JOHN 10:10 *(Jesus came so we can have abundant life)*

DAY 2: ISAIAH 12:2 *(The Lord is our strength and defense)*

DAY 3: ACTS 4:11-12 *(Salvation comes from no one but Jesus)*

DAY 4: JOHN 14:6 *(Jesus is the way, truth, and life)*

DAY 5: ACTS 16:30-33 *(Believe in Jesus to be saved)*

DAY 6: ROMANS 10:9-10 *(Declare and Believe that Jesus is Lord)*

DAY 7: REVELATION 22:17 *(Jesus offers the free gift of Salvation)*

WEEKLY COMMENTARY:

Salvation is a fancy church word that means "deliverance from harm," though I find it easier to remember it as "the act of being saved." Oftentimes when people think of Salvation, they mostly think of going to Heaven after they die.

That's only a part of Salvation. Jesus wants so much more for you and me.

In John 10:10, Jesus says that He came for us to experience life to the fullest. In other translations, the Bible says Jesus came for us to have *abundant life.*

When I think of abundance, I think of pouring so much of a liquid into a container that it overflows and comes out of the glass and onto the table. Jesus came so that you and I can have so much life that it overflows out of us and runs over onto other people. We're meant to be so full of life and joy that other people can't help but experience Jesus through us!

Life here on Earth can be full of so many amazing blessings if you allow Jesus to transform your life in a way you can enjoy. Thanks to Jesus, you are unbreakable. No stress or trauma can bring you down forever. Thanks to Jesus, every aspect of your life has an unfathomable purpose. As Christians, we can participate in God's plan of saving the entire planet! If you don't think that's amazing, you might need to check yourself for a pulse.

Jesus changes our way of thinking so that regardless of what circumstances we find ourselves in, we can experience daily joy. The love we experience and share with others as Christians is unlike anything else. When we fully live into our daily salvation, to say "Life is Good" is a massive understatement. Life's great!

Are you experiencing the Salvation that Christ died for? I heard a preacher years ago comment that Christians sometimes look like the most stressed, unhappy, and bitter people ever. He said, "I went to a church service where everyone was frowning so much it was like someone passed out lemons and that it looked like they were sucking on them for the whole service."

This week, take a step back and really live into the fact that you are saved by the blood of Jesus Christ.

REFLECTION QUESTIONS:

What does Salvation mean to you? What are all the daily benefits of being saved by Jesus?

____

____

____

____

____

____

____

In what ways can you enjoy and experience abundant life this week in your daily life?

____

____

____

____

____

____

____

PRAYER:

Jesus, thank you for dying on the cross so that I can enjoy Salvation both in Heaven and here today. Every day from you is a gift, and I am blessed in so many ways. Thank you for the many blessings you give me that I see and those that I do not. Help me live into my Salvation and share it with others around me. Amen.

WEEK 50: GIVING TO GOD

Reading Plan for NIV Scriptures:

DAY 1: 2 CORINTHIANS 9:7 *(Be a cheerful giver)*

DAY 2: 2 CORINTHIANS 8:12 *(Give out of what you have)*

DAY 3: ACTS 20:35 *(Giving is a blessing)*

DAY 4: 1 TIMOTHY 6:17-19 *(Put your hope in God, not wealth)*

DAY 5: ACTS 2:45 *(Give to anyone who has a need)*

DAY 6: PROVERBS 11:24-25 *(Generous people will prosper)*

DAY 7: MARK 12:41-44 *(Give from your heart)*

WEEKLY COMMENTARY:

A phrase that bothers me is when someone says, "I have to go to church tomorrow." This bothers me for two reasons. First of all, it is not a law to go to church. God gave us free will (I totally understand that as a teenager, your parents may, in fact, force you to go to church!) Secondly, the church is a chance to worship the most amazing and loving God Almighty! You don't "have" to go to church; you *get* to go to church! What a blessing and a privilege it is to be able to come into God's presence at church or anywhere else.

When it comes to giving back to God with our tithes and offerings, sometimes people have the same attitude. How much do I "have" to give? What's the appropriate amount to give to God so that I can feel like a good Christian? What's the least I can give?

In the Bible, Jesus tells us to give from the overflow of our hearts. It's not about what you're giving; it's about the heart behind the matter. You know this to be true in your own life. The best gifts are given out of love and from people you deeply care about. If your family member or friend gets you a gift and it's inexpensive, but they bought it just for you out of love, you're not going to disregard it because it didn't cost much, right? (I certainly hope not!) That gift has value because of the person who gave it, and I believe God views our offerings similarly.

No matter what or how much you give, God is pleased with it if it is genuine and coming from your heart.

The Bible also tells us that giving is more of a blessing than receiving. Giving back to God helps foster an attitude of gratefulness and gratitude, which will give you a holier view of the world around you. Giving to God and others freely is a way to allow the Holy Spirit to transform you into a greater person.

When we hold on to things, we slowly elevate whatever we're holding on to, giving it a level of importance that is reserved for God alone. When we allow God to work through whatever wealth we're sharing, we are creating space to witness how God provides for others which is a truly wonderful and life-changing sight to see.

This week, evaluate your offerings to God. An offering doesn't have to be money. (all though that is a big one!) Your offering can be your skills and talents or what you spend your time, attention, and thoughts on. Give back to God and see how your offerings improve your life!

REFLECTION QUESTIONS:

What are offerings that you can give to God?

____
____
____
____
____
____
____

What are ways that you can be a cheerful giver?

____
____
____
____
____
____
____

PRAYER:

God, thank you so much for all that you have given me. I give back to you out of the gratitude of my heart, and it's a small way that I can express my love and thankfulness to you. Please help me gracefully give to not just you but everyone I meet every single day. Amen.

WEEK 51: A FAILURE IS SOMETIMES AN OPTION

Reading Plan for NIV Scriptures:

DAY 1: PROVERBS 24:16 *(Rise up when you fall)*

DAY 2: ISAIAH 41:13 *(God will help you)*

DAY 3: PSALM 145:14 *(God will lift you up when you fall)*

DAY 4: REVELATION 14:12 *(We are called to remain faithful always)*

DAY 5: ROMANS 8:28 *(God works all things for His good)*

DAY 6: LAMENTATIONS 3:22 *(God's love saves us)*

DAY 7: 2 CHRONICLES 26:5 *(Gain success by seeking after God)*

WEEKLY COMMENTARY:

In an old TV show, Mission Impossible, there was a saying they would frequently say, "Failure is not an option." This was a great line for a secret agent show. The stakes of each mission were so high that the characters knew that the idea of failure meant that the world would likely end and everything would be over. So for the secret agents of Mission Impossible, failure was not an option.

In life, however, sometimes failure is an option. It's nobody's favorite option, but it's sometimes a possibility. Sometimes you may do your best and try your hardest to get that star part in the play, but the director chooses someone else. Sometimes you train all summer for tryouts and end up getting cut anyway. It's possible to be up all night studying for a test and then still make a failing grade. These aren't fun options, but it happens in life sometimes.

Sometimes the intentional decisions we make lead to a failing outcome. You make a new friend who you think is a fantastic person, but it turns out they aren't, and your relationship quickly ends with hurt feelings. You think it's a great idea to do something your parents and respected adults are advising you not to do. After you confidently commit to that action, you realize later it was a terrible mistake. Sometimes the things we do or say lead to hurt feelings or bad situations. Sometimes, even if we try not to, we will fail.

Messing up is part of life, and we can't let it define us or prevent us from moving forward. God shines through our mistakes and failures. God uses our past, even the messy parts, to help shape us and create opportunities to grow into better people. Sometimes God shines through the mistakes and moves through a circumstance in a way that everyone knows it's HIM and not YOU that prevailed. Sometimes, we fail so that God can succeed.

Whenever you face a mistake, a flaw, or a failure, don't consider it the end of your story. Keep trying if that's what you need to do, and get back up if that's what needs to happen. If it was your fault, apologize, learn from your mistakes, and let God use that moment to help you be better.

Nobody is perfect except Jesus. We're all going to mess up. Sometimes, failure's an option. That is okay. When you fail, find your strength in God.

REFLECTION QUESTIONS:

What is the scariest part of messing up for you? How can your faith in God help you deal with your fear of failing?

____

What is the most important lesson you learned through a moment that started with failure? Looking back, how was God present in that circumstance?

____

PRAYER:

God, thank you for picking me up every time I fall. Please help me not be defined by my mistakes and failures. Please help me grow and learn every day, and if I have wronged anyone recently, please show me the errors of my ways and allow me the opportunity to make it right. Amen!

WEEK 52: OUR HOME IN HEAVEN

Reading Plan for NIV Scriptures:

DAY 1: REVELATION 7:15-17 *(No pain/hunger/thirst in Heaven)*

DAY 2: PSALM 16:9-11 *(In God's full presence)*

DAY 3: REVELATION 21:4 *(There is no pain)*

DAY 4: REVELATION 21:1-3 *(God is there!)*

DAY 5: JOHN 14:1-4 *(Heaven is Home)*

DAY 6: ISAIAH 65:17-25 *(New Heaven and New Earth)*

DAY 7: REVELATION 7:9-12 *(People from all over the world in Heaven)*

WEEKLY COMMENTARY:

Have you ever been on vacation long enough that you started to really look forward to going home?

I love vacations, but there always comes the point where I long for my bed, my TV, and even my bathroom. Visiting other places is great, but those places aren't *home*. When I am away from my family, or even my house, long enough, I just start missing home.

As a Christian, you should find strength in the fact that Earth isn't your Home. Heaven is. That may seem weird because you've only ever been on Earth, but it's actually a really wonderful fact. Earth is fine, but some parts of living here aren't the best.

Bad things happen here on Earth. People get sick, get hurt, and die. Sometimes people say or do mean or terrible things. If you are reading this devotional, chances are you are in middle or high school. I know that is a time full of stress, bullies, and uncomfortable situations.

Heaven, on the other hand, not that's a different story! In Heaven, there is no pain, sin, or anything bad. In Heaven, we are made whole and pure, and with that comes the blessing of being in the *full presence* of God. Right now, because of our sins, we cannot see God's full glory, but when we are in Heaven, that will no longer be the case!

Think about the most wonderful worship experience that you have ever had. Maybe it was at a Sunday morning worship service, or maybe it was at a summer youth group camp. Maybe it was at a huge event full of people, or maybe it was outside in nature with just you and God. Either way, you experienced God, but not in all of God's glory. Now, imagine being around God's *FULL* presence. *That's* Heaven.

When you think of heaven, you should experience a sense of excitement. A sense of longing. This world has a lot of amazing blessings, and you still have a lot of good things to experience and do while you're here. Still, you should be excited about the eventuality of one day in Heaven.

As Christians, Earth is our vacation, and Heaven is our Home.

REFLECTION QUESTIONS:

What do you think Heaven will be like? What are you hoping it to be like, and what do you know to be true about Heaven?

____

____

____

____

____

____

____

____

What are some questions or maybe even some fears or insecurities you have about the idea of Heaven? (Feel free to discuss these with a trusted Christian role model this week!)

____

____

____

____

____

____

____

____

PRAYER:

God, thank you so much for the hope that I have in Heaven. Thank you so much for the glorious home that you have created for me. Thank you for all the wonderful things you have blessed me with in this life to remind me of what Heaven is like, and thank you for being with me during the temporary but tough parts of this world. You are an amazing God, and I love you! Amen.

CONCLUSION

It wasn't intentional, but a word that kept showing up in these devotionals is Shine. Within many of the topics and prayers, the statement "Let God shine through you" was written. Jesus calls us the lamps that shine His light on others, especially in the darkest place. We shine Jesus's light by loving others, sharing His word, and doing our best to live the holiest lives possible.

I hope these devotionals have been a light to you and that the Holy Spirit has shone through these words to impact you and help you. I pray that God used these devotionals and the power of daily Scripture to help transform you into someone a little better than you were when you first opened this book. Even if this book has helped you grow in your faith, even a little bit, I consider it a strong success.

Now it's your turn to go and continue to be a light in the lives of everyone you come into contact with. Share Jesus with them and point them to a God that unconditionally loves them and wants a real relationship with them, just like He wants with you.

Additionally, your relationship with God doesn't end after you put this book down. Continue to grow and be in a community with God, your community, and those outside your community. Share Jesus's love and worship God in everything you do. This is how you live your best possible life.

And what a blessing that life is!

Now go and shine Christ's light everywhere you go.

www.ingramcontent.com/pod-product-compliance
Lightning Source LLC
LaVergne TN
LVHW021250210726
843527LV00004B/242